PRESENTED TO

_____

BY

_____

DATE

_____

WHAT DOES GOD REALLY PROMISE?

101 QUESTIONS AND ANSWERS ABOUT GOD'S PROMISES, THE CHURCH, AND THE FUTURE

WRITTEN BY: *Carolyn Larsen*

ILLUSTRATED BY: *Amylee Weeks*

TYNDALE MOMENTUM

An Imprint of
Tyndale House Publishers, Inc.

Visit Tyndale online at www.tyndale.com.

Visit the author's website at www.carolynlarsen.com.

Visit the illustrator's website at www.amyleeweeks.com.

Tyndale Momentum and the Tyndale Momentum logo are registered trademarks of Tyndale House Publishers, Inc. Tyndale Momentum is an imprint of Tyndale House Publishers, Inc., Carol Stream, Illinois.

What Does God Really Promise?: 101 Questions and Answers about God's Promises, the Church, and the Future

Text copyright © 2016 by Carolyn Larsen. All rights reserved.

Illustrations copyright © Amylee Weeks

Designed by Jennifer Ghionzoli

Published in association with Educational Publishing Concepts, PO Box 655, Wheaton, IL 60187.

ISBN 978-1-4964-1176-1

Printed in China

22	21	20	19	18	17	16
7	6	5	4	3	2	1

INTRODUCTION

Faith is belief or confidence in something, even when the object of faith cannot be fully grasped in the physical realm. A relationship with God is based on faith in him. It's a growth process of learning to accept and appreciate his grace, mercy, and love. The "instruction manual" God has given us—the Bible—helps us understand who God is and shows us how to live for him, obey him, trust him, and love him. But even with this source of amazing help and the commitment to engage in life with God through faith, we sometimes have questions.

Questions aren't wrong. In fact, they're helpful because they express a desire to learn and understand. However, it's important to search for answers to your questions from a reliable source that is true to Scripture. *What Does God Really Promise?* answers 101 frequently asked questions that are common to those who are investigating faith in Jesus Christ.

Part one explores the loving promises God has made to his children. Part two relates to the church Jesus established—what he intended it to be, its differing forms of expression, and why it sometimes fails but more often succeeds in fulfilling his purposes. And part three delves into what the future holds for those who love God and what will happen to those who reject him. It is our hope that this book will help answer some of your questions and pave the way for a strong faith in God.

ACKNOWLEDGMENTS

Writing a book like this one carries with it the responsibility to be true to Scripture, to not mislead readers, and to honor and revere God. It is not something that can be accomplished alone. So I wish to thank the wonderful people at Tyndale House Publishers for their wisdom, input, and support. I appreciate Tyndale's standard of excellence and desire to honor God in every book they publish. Thank you, Anisa Baker and Becky Brandvik, for your vision for this book. Thank you to Anne Christian Buchanan for your attention to detail and "big picture" plan. It's been a privilege to work with all of you.

Carolyn Larsen

* Part 1 *

QUESTIONS AND ANSWERS
ABOUT GOD'S
PROMISES

Q. WHAT DOES GOD REALLY PROMISE?

How can I know what his promises are? Does he give a list of them in the Bible?

A. The Bible is filled with hundreds of God's promises for his people. These promises are not listed all together in one place but are found throughout God's Word. Though given at different times and for different situations, many still apply today and are for everyone who trusts in him—including you!

You can discover the richness of these promises by reading through the Bible—which is a great idea anyway. Another way is to look for study books that feature compiled lists of God's promises. These lists will most likely give the specific Bible reference for each promise. Be sure to read the entire surrounding passage so you can understand its context and determine if the promise is applicable to you, as many are! Most of all, as you read the promises, let your heart be saturated with God's love, which shines through all of his promises.

Because of his glory and excellence, he has given us great and precious promises. These are the promises that enable you to share his divine nature and escape the world's corruption caused by human desires. 2 PETER 1:4

Q. WHAT DOES GOD PROMISE FOR ME PERSONALLY?

Is one promise more important than all the others?

A. When considering this, it's good to keep in mind that all of God's promises are important because they all reflect God's amazing love for you.

Certainly one of the most important promises, if not *the* most important, is God's promise to forgive your sins—and not just for the moment, but to forget them entirely by wiping them out of his memory (Isaiah 43:25). God promises that when you come to him and confess your sins, you'll get a clean start on a new life. That's major!

As part of that new life, there are other wonderful promises that follow. For example, God will supply all your needs. Everything you need is on God's radar, and he will take care of it. Yet another is that God will give you victory over death. When you breathe your last on this earth, your life will not be over because you will live eternally in heaven with him.

Those are just three of the wonderful biblical promises that can apply to you personally. Whichever of these promises speaks most dearly to your heart, know that each one reflects God's deep, deep love for you.

This same God who takes care of me will supply all your needs from his glorious riches, which have been given to us in Christ Jesus. PHILIPPIANS 4:19

Q. CAN I TRUST GOD TO KEEP HIS PROMISES?

God's promises sound wonderful, but how do I know he will keep those promises and not let me down?

A. The key to trusting God's promises is to look at his character. He is loving and unchanging, the God of all truth. He is also all-powerful, which means he has the ability to keep all the promises he makes.

You need to realize, however, that God operates according to his own timetable—not yours or mine. He does exactly what he says he will do, but not necessarily when we think he should. God sees the big picture and knows when the time is right to fulfill what he has spoken.

Scripture is filled with stories of how God kept his promises of protection and provision for his people, sometimes in miraculous ways. If you're feeling uneasy about trusting God's promises, a good place to start is the book of Exodus, which recounts how God delivered his people out of slavery in Egypt. Speaking with other Christians helps as well. Hearing their accounts of God's faithfulness can boost your own faith. Look at your past, too, and ask God to help you see the ways he has kept his promises. God loves you more deeply than you can imagine. You can trust him to keep his word to you.

○ ○ ○ ○ ○ ● ○ ○ ○ ○ ○ ○ ○ ○ ○ ○ ● ● ○ ○ ○ ○ ○ ○ ● ○ ○

Let us hold tightly without wavering to the hope we affirm, for God can be trusted to keep his promise. HEBREWS 10:23

Q. ARE GOD'S PROMISES UNCONDITIONAL?

Will God keep them no matter what I do?

A. Some of God's promises are unconditional, meaning they do not depend on human choices or behavior. Instead, they are based purely on God's plan and his character. For instance, after the great Flood, God promised he would never again destroy the earth with a deluge. He also promised there will be a day when Jesus returns and Satan pays for his rebellion. Nothing we do or don't do will change the outcome of these promises.

But most promises in the Bible *do* have a condition attached—"If you do this, then I will do that." If you obey God, he will bless you, though sometimes not in the way you were hoping or expecting. If you seek his will, he will guide you. If you trust him, he will protect your heart. God desires that we do things his way in order to benefit from his blessings. That's why he puts conditions on many of his promises—to motivate us to live in a way that brings us closer to him.

○ ○ ○ ○ ○ ○ ○ ○ ○ ○ ● ○ ● ○ ○ ○ ○ ○ ○ ○ ○ ● ○ ○ ○ ● ○ ○

I command you this day to love the LORD your God and to keep his commands. . . . If you do this, you will live and multiply, and the LORD your God will bless you.   DEUTERONOMY 30:16

Q. WHAT IS A COVENANT PROMISE?

Is a covenant the same as a promise?

A. A covenant is a special kind of promise. It's a legal term referring to a formal and binding agreement between two parties. The Bible contains several examples of covenants made between God and his people.

There is a pattern to how covenant promises are made in the Bible. First God establishes who he is and the authority he has, and he states what he plans to do. Then he usually gives a list of what people must do in order for the promise to be kept (obey God, honor him, respect him). He explains the rewards for obeying him and the consequences for disobeying. In other words, most of the covenants in the Bible are *conditional*. They require a response from those with whom God makes his covenant.

Another word for covenant is *testament*. The two parts of the Christian Bible, the Old Testament and the New Testament, refer to the two most important covenants in the Bible—the covenant between God and the Israelites and the fulfillment and renewal of that covenant through the atoning sacrifice of Jesus the Messiah.

- -

Now if you will obey me and keep my covenant, you will be my own special treasure from among all the peoples on earth; for all the earth belongs to me. EXODUS 19:5

Q. DOES GOD PROMISE ONLY GOOD THINGS?

Or does he promise bad things too?

A. The flip side of a conditional promise is a warning or curse. And while God does promise many wonderful things to those who love and obey him, he also prescribes consequences for those who don't.

God is not being cruel or vindictive in warning people of the consequences of breaking his laws. He has great love for the people he created and doesn't want anything bad to happen to them. But God has also given us free will, which means we can always choose to disobey him and live outside his laws. And that choice has built-in negative consequences: If we insist on choosing sin and evil instead of living a life that is pleasing to him, then we will face a painful outcome.

- -

Look, today I am giving you the choice between a blessing and a curse! You will be blessed if you obey the commands of the LORD your God that I am giving you today. But you will be cursed if you reject the commands of the LORD your God and turn away from him. DEUTERONOMY 11:26-28

Q. WHAT IS THE FIRST PROMISE GIVEN IN THE BIBLE?

Is it something wonderful?

A. The first promise in the Bible is a conditional one, given in the form of a warning. God placed the first man and woman in a beautiful garden where they had everything they needed. He gave them permission to freely eat the fruit from every tree in the Garden except one—the "tree of the knowledge of good and evil." If they ate fruit from that tree, God promised they would die!

You probably know the rest of that story. Satan, the rebellious fallen angel, took the form of a serpent to tempt Adam and Eve. He convinced Eve to eat the fruit, and she convinced Adam to also try it. God had no choice but to keep his promise and evict them from the perfect Garden—a death sentence for Adam and Eve and all humankind. Fortunately, God didn't give up on his disobedient children. One of his next promises was that Eve's offspring would strike the serpent's head. And that's exactly what happened. Thousands of years later, Jesus died on the cross to provide a way for people to escape Satan's temptations and live in harmony with God. He made many more promises . . . and kept them!

When Adam sinned, sin entered the world. Adam's sin brought death, so death spread to everyone, for everyone sinned.

ROMANS 5:12

Q. WHAT ARE SOME BIBLICAL PROMISES GOD MADE—AND KEPT?

And why do they matter for my life?

A. The history of God's promises is important to know because it tells us so much about God's character and his patient, persistent love. Here are just three of the promises God made and kept as recorded in the Old Testament:

- After the Flood wiped out the entire world except for Noah's family and the animals on the ark, God promised never to destroy the world by water again. He has kept that promise to this day.

- God told Abraham he would be the father of a great nation, with descendants as numerous as the stars in the sky. But Abraham and his wife, Sarah, had no children! Finally, in their old age, they bore a son named Isaac, the ancestor of the Israelites.

- When the Israelites were enslaved in Egypt, God commissioned Moses to lead them to freedom and promised them a beautiful land of their own. After many years wandering through the desert, God's people finally settled in the beautiful land that today is called Israel.

Look, I am giving all this land to you! Go in and occupy it, for it is the land the LORD swore to give to your ancestors Abraham, Isaac, and Jacob, and to all their descendants. DEUTERONOMY 1:8

Q. WHAT IS THE MOST IMPORTANT PROMISE GOD HAS MADE?

Does this promise apply to me?

A. The most important promise God has made is to redeem humanity from sin. It is given throughout the Old Testament in the form of prophecies that grow more and more specific. God would send a Messiah (which means "anointed one")—a descendant of King David who would be born in Bethlehem. He would be tortured and killed, but in the process he would reverse the curse of sin and death that haunted humanity.

By the time Jesus lived, God's people were eagerly awaiting the promised Messiah, though many had forgotten the prophecies about his suffering and death. They thought he would be a political figure who would liberate them from the occupying Roman government. Instead they got a Messiah—God in human form—who first showed them how to live, then died on the cross to make atonement for sin. And rising to life again, Jesus brought ultimate deliverance by defeating death. God's most important promise, in other words, was given to all of us. It was Jesus!

○ ○ ○ ○ ○ ● ○ ○ ○ ○ ● ● ○ ○ ● ○ ○ ● ● ● ○ ○ ○ ○ ○ ● ○ ○

He was pierced for our rebellion, crushed for our sins. He was beaten so we could be whole. . . . We have left God's paths to follow our own. Yet the LORD laid on him the sins of us all.

ISAIAH 53:5-6

Q. WHAT DID JESUS PROMISE HIS DISCIPLES BEFORE HE DIED?

He told them he was going to die, right? Did he give them any hope to hold on to?

A. Jesus knew he was going to be killed, and he wanted to prepare his disciples for what would happen. So he gave them a series of promises to cling to in the midst of their confusion and grief. The disciples didn't completely understand them at the time, but they did later. Here are just a few of the promises Jesus gave them before he died:

- He would die and be raised back to life
- He would prepare a place for them in heaven
- He would send the Holy Spirit to dwell in them, to comfort and help them
- He would always be with them, no matter what

Every one of these promises came true for the disciples, and they still hold true for believers today. We can be confident that the Holy Spirit dwells within us, that Jesus is preparing a place for us in heaven, that we will see him in person someday, and that he is always with us, even in the midst of our everyday troubles.

Be sure of this: I am with you always, even to the end of the age.
MATTHEW 28:20

Q. IF GOD PROMISES TO SUPPLY ALL OUR NEEDS, WHY ARE SOME CHRISTIANS STILL NEEDY?

I know of some who are hungry or persecuted—and I have unmet needs too!

A. God does keep his promise to meet our needs. The trouble is, we don't always know what our real needs are! Many things we ask God for are "wants," not needs—and God knows the difference.

God knows what will help each of us grow into the person we have the potential to be. He knows what circumstances will teach us how to lean on him and trust him. And some of these situations may be different from what we would choose. But we never have to go through these situations alone! God is always with us—guiding, strengthening, teaching, and loving—which is what we need most of all.

God also works through us to meet others' needs. Jesus said that when we feed the hungry, visit the lonely, and clothe the needy, we are actually connecting with him. In the process of meeting needs, we'll find our own deepest needs are met as well.

The King will say, "I tell you the truth, when you did it to one of the least of these my brothers and sisters, you were doing it to me!"

MATTHEW 25:40

Q. DOES GOD PROMISE ME HAPPINESS?

If he does, why do I often feel sad or upset?

A. God does not promise us happiness in the sense that the world defines it. He does not guarantee a life free from problems and disappointments or promise that we will always have everything we want. He does not tell us to expect overwhelming success or an easy life. For Christians, as for all humans, happiness is a delightful but fleeting emotional experience. There's nothing wrong with it—after all, God created our emotions too—but continual happiness is not a given in the Christian life.

What God *does* promise is to be with us through problems and disappointments—to comfort us, teach us, and guide us through them. He promises we will have all we need (as opposed to all we want) and that he will help us in all we attempt to do if we seek his guidance. God may not promise happiness, but he does promise joy, a deep gladness that is not dependent on external circumstances. Joy comes when we seek to live for God, honoring him and growing in Christlike character. That's a promise!

Though you do not see him now, you trust him; and you rejoice with a glorious, inexpressible joy. The reward for trusting him will be the salvation of your souls. 1 PETER 1:8-9

Q. DOES GOD PROMISE TO ALWAYS LOVE ME?

When bad things happen, I don't feel very loved.

A. God's love for you is beyond comprehension. He sent his only Son from heaven to earth to teach us how to live abundantly and sacrifice his own life to offer us a personal relationship with him. That's a very deep love. He wouldn't walk away from that love when he has paid so great a price for it. God loves the whole of humankind, as John 3:16 states, but he also loves you personally. You could substitute your own name into the verse, and it would still be just as true: "This is how God loved _____: He gave his one and only Son so that_____ will not perish but have eternal life."

Yes, there may be times when you don't "feel" loved because of difficulties and hardships. *Where is God's love then?* you may wonder. Though it may sound trite, the answer is, "Right there with you." His love is demonstrated by his presence as he comforts, strengthens, and teaches you. God doesn't keep you from hard times. He grows you through them. And in the process he always, always loves you!

○ ○ ○ ○ ○ ● ○ ○ ○ ○ ● ○ ○ ○ ○ ○ ● ● ○ ○ ○ ○ ● ○ ○ ○

I have loved you, my people, with an everlasting love. With unfailing love I have drawn you to myself. JEREMIAH 31:3

Q. DOES GOD PROMISE TO KEEP ME SAFE?

Will he keep me from getting a horrible illness or having an accident?

A. Scripture says that God will protect us and keep us safe. But understanding this requires knowing what is truly important to God—as opposed to what may be important to us.

You probably know, either from your own experiences or those of other people, that God does not always keep his followers from illness, grief, physical injury, or any of the dangers that are common to life in this world. Christians get sick, suffer hurt, and die from illness or injuries. They are not exempt from painful loss.

So what does God's promise of protection mean? His protection is focused on our souls because that's the most important aspect of who we are. The soul is eternal, while the physical life we're experiencing now is temporary. His promise of guidance and protection is designed to help us journey through the world without giving in to Satan and his efforts to pull us away from God. If we trust God, turn to him, lean on him, and call on him, he promises to keep our souls safe. In some circumstances, he may also choose to protect us from physical or emotional harm.

* * *

The LORD keeps you from all harm and watches over your life.

PSALM 121:7

Q. IN WHAT WAYS DOES GOD PROMISE TO PROTECT ME?

How exactly does God protect my soul from danger?

A. Make no mistake—Satan will do anything he can to get us to turn our backs on God. He's a consummate liar and the enemy of our souls. The Bible even says that he stalks about like a hungry lion, "looking for someone to devour" (1 Peter 5:8).

The good news is that God has promised to protect us from Satan's schemes and to keep our souls safe from harm. If we ask God for his help and protection and stay close to him, he will give us the discernment to recognize temptation and the strength to resist it. He will give us wisdom for making right choices. He will help us understand the meaning of Scripture.

And although God doesn't promise to protect us from the physical and emotional struggles and dangers of this life—illness, grief, physical injury, even death—he does promise to walk through them with us. He uses Scripture, other people, and the nudging of his Holy Spirit to strengthen and encourage us, help us learn from what happens, and show us love. With God, we are never alone.

- -

I hold you by your right hand—I, the LORD your God. And I say to you, "Don't be afraid. I am here to help you."   ISAIAH 41:13

Q. WHAT DOES GOD PROMISE ABOUT SUFFERING?

Will he bring something good from my pain?

A. God promises that you *will* have pain in your life. Because of sin, suffering is just a built-in part of living in our world. Some of it is deserved—we suffer because of wrong or harmful choices we make. But a lot of it can seem just plain cruel and senseless.

Why it happens is a mystery that has bothered people for centuries, and only God knows the full answer. But his Word does contain some ideas that can help us understand the reasoning a little better.

According to the Bible, pain is a given in this world—but God is bigger than the world. He can use our suffering—deserved or undeserved—to teach us and make us stronger and more compassionate. And he promises that if we trust in him, our suffering will be temporary.

Suffering is never fun. It can make us feel angry or hopeless. But it also brings a choice: to let the pain overwhelm us or to give it up to God and lean on him. If we choose the latter, we will learn that no matter what causes our suffering, God is with us through it.

- -

[Jesus said,] "Here on earth you will have many trials and sorrows. But take heart, because I have overcome the world."

JOHN 16:33

Q. CAN GOD'S PROMISES HELP ME MAKE THE RIGHT DECISIONS?

And does this mean I'll never make wrong ones?

A. God does promise us guidance, so yes, his promises will help us make good decisions. But before God's promises can help us, we must know what they are! We do this by spending time in his Word, the Bible—not just reading it, but studying it to understand exactly what it says. And then we must do what it says! If we don't bother to learn God's promises or if we don't heed his commandments, how can we expect to benefit from his guidance?

If we study the Bible and do our best to obey its teachings, will we always make good decisions? Of course not. Because of sin and our limited understanding, we all make mistakes and bad choices from time to time. But sincerely seeking God's guidance still helps a lot. When you aren't sure what to do, ask for God's help. Pray for wisdom, search the Scriptures, seek wise counsel, and try to stay open to the "nudges" of the Holy Spirit. (The more you do this, the more easily you'll recognize them.) Then trust God to do what he has promised—to guide you toward making the right choices.

Your laws please me; they give me wise advice.   PSALM 119:24

Q. DOES GOD PROMISE TO HELP ME RESIST TEMPTATION?

I'm not strong enough to fight temptation on my own. Will he help me?

A. Everyone on earth has faced temptation, even Jesus. But Jesus is the only human being who never gave in to temptation. The rest of us have sinned. And none of us are strong enough to resist temptation on our own—at least not on a consistent basis.

Satan is a master at temptation. He knows our weaknesses, the places where he can bring us down most easily. And he will continually wave temptation in front of us until we either give in or call on God's strength to push the temptation away.

Will God help you overcome temptation? Yes, but first remember to ask for his help. You must be an active participant in the process—staying in his Word, obeying his commands, trusting in his strength. Even then, you will probably give in to temptation from time to time. If that happens, remember that you can come to him, confess your lapse, receive forgiveness, and start again fresh.

The temptations in your life are no different from what others experience. And God is faithful. He will not allow the temptation to be more than you can stand. When you are tempted, he will show you a way out so that you can endure. 1 CORINTHIANS 10:13

Q. WHY DOESN'T GOD PROMISE TO TELL ME EXACTLY WHAT TO DO?

Wouldn't it be easier if he just told me what to do so I didn't have to figure it out?

A. Think about it: Not having to make decisions might be easier for a while, but would you actually be happy? Wouldn't you begin to feel like a puppet whose every move is controlled by a puppeteer? And wouldn't you then begin to resent God?

God, in his wisdom, has given us all the gift of free will. That means we can choose to follow him or not, to obey him or not, to study his Word and grow stronger in faith or to ignore him and do things our way. And though God doesn't tell us exactly what to do or force us to do it, he does offer help and guidance. When we choose obedience and ask for his help in following through, he promises to give it. When we make mistakes and turn to him for forgiveness, he promises to give that too. Best of all, these choices bring us closer to God. Free will isn't always easy, but it's the only way for us to be in relationship with God—because a real relationship must be chosen, not forced.

○ ○ ○ ○ ○ ● ○ ○ ○ ○ ● ○ ○ ○ ○ ○ ○ ● ○ ● ● ○ ○ ○ ○ ○ ● ○ ○

Let God transform you into a new person by changing the way you think. Then you will learn to know God's will for you, which is good and pleasing and perfect. ROMANS 12:2

Q. WHAT DOES GOD PROMISE ABOUT HONORING MY PARENTS?

And what exactly does it mean to honor them?

A. God takes joy when we honor our parents, and he promises a life of fruitfulness and longevity to those who do. Honoring your parents means obeying them when you are young and continuing to show them kindness and respect once you are grown. Parents are not perfect, and their actions or choices may have been hurtful at some point in your life, but this does not mean you should dishonor them in return. God is pleased when you show love to them in spite of any wrongs you may have suffered.

But does God really promise a long life? We all know people who treated their parents with great honor and still died at a young age. That was even true of Jesus! So it makes more sense to think of the promise as a general principle: Those who honor their parents are *more likely* to live well and long than those who don't. If you have the habit of respecting those who raise you, you are more likely to have self-discipline and good relationships with God and others—characteristics of a positive, healthy lifestyle that promotes a long and good life.

○ ○ ○ ○ ○ ○ ○ ○ ● ● ○ ○ ○ ○ ○ ○ ○ ○ ○ ○ ● ○ ○ ○ ○ ○ ○

If you honor your father and mother, "things will go well for you, and you will have a long life on the earth." EPHESIANS 6:3

Q. DOES GOD PROMISE TO ANSWER ALL MY PRAYERS?

Sometimes it doesn't seem like anything happens when I pray.

A. God wants us to pray, invites us to pray, and commands us to pray. He wouldn't put such an emphasis on praying if he didn't intend to answer our prayers.

We all experience times when we pray and nothing seems to happen. That doesn't mean God isn't listening! It just means we're having trouble "hearing" the answer—perhaps because it's not the one we're looking for.

God doesn't respond to every prayer with "Yes, let me take care of that right this moment." Sometimes his answer is a plain and simple no—because what we ask for is not good for us or for someone else. And sometimes his answer is "Not right now"—perhaps because he is waiting for us to learn something or to recognize his work in the situation.

Often it's easier to recognize God's answers in retrospect. We may feel God isn't doing anything in the moment, but later when we look back, we'll see amazing answers to our prayers. So we need to keep our eyes and hearts open and practice patience to appreciate all the surprising ways he responds to us.

If we look forward to something we don't yet have, we must wait patiently and confidently. ROMANS 8:25

Q. WHY DON'T I FEEL PEACEFUL WHEN GOD HAS PROMISED ME PEACE?

I'm often confused or upset instead of calm and confident.

A. God wants all of us to be able to live with a peaceful spirit, trusting him with what happens in our lives and with the unknown future. But such peace doesn't come naturally to most of us, so this promise involves a learning curve. We must practice and develop our "trust muscles." We do this by staying in constant conversation with God; by studying and meditating on Scripture and seeking his guidance with our whole hearts; by spending time with Christians who display this quality in their lives (God's peace is contagious!); and by practicing obedience—daring to do what we think God wants even when we're scared or unsure.

And no, we won't always be at peace—not as long as we are living in this flawed, sinful world. But the more we learn to trust, the more of God's perfect peace we will experience. And the more we taste that peace, the more we will be motivated to trust!

You [God] will keep in perfect peace all who trust in you, all whose thoughts are fixed on you! ISAIAH 26:3

Q. WHAT DOES GOD PROMISE TO THOSE WHO STUDY THE BIBLE?

Are there rewards for those who spend time reading God's Word?

A. God promises great rewards for those who study his Word. The Bible is a living source of God's love, strength, help, and guidance. But to access those good things, we have to spend time reading, studying, and meditating on what it says. The more we do that, the better we will know him and the more we will understand his great love for us.

Knowing the truths of the Bible draws us closer to God and equips us for anything that might come our way in life. It gives us God's strength for fighting off Satan's attacks. It teaches us how to obey God and live peacefully with others. It instills patience and compassion as we learn to love people the way God does. It offers a wealth of God's wisdom for making decisions. The reward for studying God's Word is that we will have all the information we need to flourish as Christ followers.

○ ○ ○ ○ ○ ● ○ ○ ○ ○ ● ○ ○ ○ ○ ○ ○ ● ● ○ ○ ○ ○ ○ ● ○ ○

All Scripture is inspired by God and is useful to teach us what is true and to make us realize what is wrong in our lives. It corrects us when we are wrong and teaches us to do what is right. God uses it to prepare and equip his people to do every good work.

2 TIMOTHY 3:16-17

Q. DOES GOD PROMISE ME WEALTH AND PROSPERITY?

I've heard people say that if I have enough faith, I'll receive financial blessings. How does that work?

A. It doesn't—at least not the way some people explain it! The idea that God gives monetary rewards for faith is called "the prosperity gospel," and it's not true to the spirit of Scripture. It makes the life of faith all about us instead of about God. There are plenty of people who have great faith, yet struggle financially all their lives.

God does promise blessings in reward for faith, but those are the blessings of growing closer to God and having our faith and trust in him grow deeper. If material prosperity will help accomplish that, God *may* provide that. But he grants all blessings according to his purposes. There is absolutely no guarantee that faith will result in wealth.

God cares about our relationship with him. He cares about our lives and our eternity with him. He wants us to make those things our focus instead of worldly or financial success.

◦ ◦

Don't love money; be satisfied with what you have. For God has said, "I will never fail you. I will never abandon you."

HEBREWS 13:5

Q. WHAT ARE GOD'S PROMISES WHEN I GIVE GENEROUSLY TO HIS WORK?

God doesn't need my money, does he?

A. No, God doesn't need money, but he wants our hearts—and our hearts are often tied up with our possessions. That's why money is such a frequent topic in the Bible. The Bible teaches that we should be generous with our possessions and give a portion of what we receive to God's work. This includes our time and talents as well. And when we give generously, God promises us blessings. In fact, he promises that we'll receive much, much more than we give.

That's not to say we should give just so we will get something in return! We are not "buying" God's blessings but acknowledging God's gifts and the opportunity to be part of what he is doing in the world. And we can't dictate the *form* the blessings will take—financial, emotional, or spiritual. But when we give out of gratitude and obedience, acknowledging that everything we have comes from God in the first place, we can expect good things to happen.

"Bring all the tithes into the storehouse so there will be enough food in my Temple. If you do," says the LORD, . . . *"I will pour out a blessing so great you won't have enough room to take it in! Try it! Put me to the test!"* MALACHI 3:10

Q. DOES GOD PROMISE TO GIVE ME FAITH?

I know that faith in God is important, but I'm not sure how I get it—or even what it is.

A. Faith is believing and trusting in something without absolute proof that the object of your belief is real. It is also a manifestation of your devotion to God, because the Bible tells us it's impossible to please God without faith. But Scripture makes it clear that faith is not something we can create on our own, even by praying or studying. Faith is a gift from God, and it's a gift he wants to give us!

Even if we have only the tiniest suspicion that God might be real, he can work with it. He invites us to test that little bit of faith by living as if we truly believe in him—and then watching to see what happens. Scripture is filled with examples of people who trusted God for guidance, protection, healing, and restoration. These stories teach us about the power of faith in difficult circumstances. When our faith in God is tested, it grows stronger because we see proof of God's caring presence in our lives.

- -

This faith was given to you because of the justice and fairness of Jesus Christ, our God and Savior. 2 PETER 1:1

Q. WHAT DOES GOD PROMISE ABOUT MY FUTURE?

Does he have it all planned out? Will he make it clear?

A. God does have a plan—both a general one that applies to all of us and a specific one for each person. God's general plan for all of us is that we come to know him through a personal relationship with Jesus. What matters most is to seek after him, obey him, serve him, use the gifts and talents he has given us, and love him more deeply with every passing day.

But what about God's plan for us as individuals? God wants us to be serious about discerning his will and following it. But he doesn't spell it out for us. We must seek God's wisdom by praying earnestly and reading his Word with the purpose of hearing his direction for our lives. But we don't need to worry that a wrong decision on our part will sabotage everything. God is infinitely creative, and he can fit even our mistakes into his plan. Our part is to trust him, do our best to receive his guidance, and then move ahead, confident he will help us make necessary adjustments along the way.

My child, eat honey, for it is good, and the honeycomb is sweet to the taste. In the same way, wisdom is sweet to your soul. If you find it, you will have a bright future, and your hopes will not be cut short. PROVERBS 24:13-14

Q. SHOULD GOD'S PROMISES AFFECT THE WAY I LIVE?

Can't I just do what I want, then ask God to forgive me if necessary?

A. God's promise of forgiveness is an amazing thing. Scripture states very clearly that when we confess our sins to God, he forgives us. In fact, he actually wipes those sins from his memory. But that's not an excuse to do whatever we want, presuming that we can just be forgiven later.

The goal of a life lived with God is to become more like Jesus. God's promise of forgiveness is given within that larger context—and it cost him the life of his only Son. If we treat forgiveness as a license to keep on sinning, we miss the whole point, hurting others and ourselves and insulting God in the process!

Our desire should always be to obey God's commands and please him by the way we live. It's a given that we will mess up and need forgiveness. But the only way to truly please God and claim his blessings is through obedience.

Since God's grace has set us free . . . does that mean we can go on sinning? Of course not! Don't you realize that you become the slave of whatever you choose to obey? You can be a slave to sin, which leads to death, or you can choose to obey God, which leads to righteous living.   ROMANS 6:15-16

Q. WHAT DOES GOD'S PROMISE OF ETERNAL LIFE MEAN?

I don't understand how living forever is even possible. Is it too good to be true?

A. The bodies we have now eventually die, but the part of us that is not physical—the soul and spirit—lives on after death.

God promises we will have eternal life with him if we commit our lives to Jesus, believing that he took the punishment for our sins when he died on the cross. He was raised back to life by the power of God, ascended to his Father in heaven, and will one day return to usher in a new era of justice and peace. If we put our trust in Jesus, we will be part of that remarkable future: When he returns, he will resurrect our physical bodies and transform them into glorious bodies that will never die again. We will live with him forever! If we deny him, however, we will be condemned to eternal death in hell, separated for all time from the God who gives life. The choice is ours to make, and it has far-reaching consequences: We are choosing where we will spend eternity.

○ ○ ○ ○ ○ ● ○ ○ ○ ○ ○ ○ ○ ○ ○ ● ○ ● ●○ ○ ○ ○ ○ ○ ● ○ ○

We are citizens of heaven, where the Lord Jesus Christ lives. And we are eagerly waiting for him to return as our Savior. He will take our weak mortal bodies and change them into glorious bodies like his own. PHILIPPIANS 3:20-21

Q. WHAT IS THE LAST PROMISE IN THE BIBLE?

And why did God promise it last?

A. The last promise given in the Bible is one of the most hopeful and wonderful promises of all. In the next-to-last verse of the book of Revelation, Jesus says, "I am coming soon!" And yes, it has been nearly two thousand years since he said that, but God's sense of time is not the same as ours. We can take heart that it *will* happen, though. Jesus said so!

However difficult our lives may be, however messed up the world seems, however hopeless we may feel, we can hold on to that promise: Jesus is coming back. And when he does, he will make everything new. All the sin and all the sadness will vanish. Our hope is in his return, and our future is with him, so we don't have to let the struggles and difficulties of life get us down.

Why did God arrange for this to be the last promise we read in the Bible? Perhaps it's because he wants us to remember it. So after reading all of his other promises in the Bible, you can always return to this hopeful last word. No matter what else happens, Jesus is coming soon!

∘ ° ∘ ∘ ∘ ∘ ∘ ∘ ⊙ ∘ ∘ • ∘ ⊙ ∘ ∘ ∘ ∘ ∘ ∘ ∘ ∘ ∘ • ∘ ∘ ° ∘ ∘

He who is the faithful witness to all these things says, "Yes, I am coming soon!" Amen! Come, Lord Jesus!   REVELATION 22:20

Part 2

QUESTIONS AND ANSWERS ABOUT GOD'S CHURCH

Q. WHAT DID JESUS MEAN WHEN HE SAID HE WAS BUILDING HIS CHURCH ON A ROCK?

Was he talking about an actual stone?

A. Jesus was speaking to his disciple Simon when he spoke those words. Jesus had asked his disciples what they thought of him—who they thought he was. And Simon, who tended to be impulsive, immediately blurted out, "You are the Messiah, the Son of the living God."

Bingo! Simon nailed it. Jesus immediately blessed him and said, "You are Peter (which means 'rock'), and upon this rock I will build my church." In other words, the future church would consist of those with solid belief that Jesus was God's Son, sent to redeem the world from sin.

For the rest of his life, Simon would be known as Peter. Although he would remain impulsive and make mistakes, he would also be a key figure in founding the church. He would even write two letters that are now included in the New Testament of the Bible.

Jesus replied, "You are blessed, Simon son of John, because my Father in heaven has revealed this to you. You did not learn this from any human being. Now I say to you that you are Peter (which means 'rock'), and upon this rock I will build my church, and all the powers of hell will not conquer it. And I will give you the keys of the Kingdom of Heaven." MATTHEW 16:17-19

Q. HOW AND WHEN DID THE CHURCH GET STARTED?

Did Jesus or his followers start it?

A. In a sense, the first New Testament church was the group of followers who traveled with Jesus and shared life with him. But its official birth happened several weeks after Jesus was resurrected and took place in Jerusalem during the feast of Pentecost.

Jesus' disciples were gathered together when the Holy Spirit descended on them with a loud sound like a rush of wind. Flames appeared above everyone's heads, and suddenly they could speak in different languages. God's people who lived in foreign lands were in Jerusalem for Pentecost, and when they heard the disciples speaking in their own languages, they ran to see what was happening. Peter told them the Good News about Jesus, and more than three thousand people came to believe in him that day! After that, Christians began meeting together regularly and traveling to spread the news about Jesus to other cities. That was the beginning of the church as we know it.

All the believers devoted themselves to the apostles' teaching . . . and to prayer. . . . They worshiped together at the Temple each day . . . and shared their meals with great joy and generosity. . . . And each day the Lord added to their fellowship those who were being saved. ACTS 2:42, 46-47

Q. WHY IS THE CHURCH CALLED "THE BODY OF CHRIST"?

It's not like his physical body, is it?

A. When Jesus Christ left heaven and came to earth, he took on a physical human body that suffered death so our sins could be forgiven. But three days after his crucifixion, Jesus appeared to his disciples—fully and gloriously alive! Before returning to heaven, Jesus commissioned them to continue his work of sharing the message of God's love. That may be one reason the apostle Paul called the church "the body of Christ." It is continuing the work Jesus began in his physical body when he was here on earth.

The church is made up of people who are connected to Christ through their salvation and through the Holy Spirit who dwells within them. That is another reason the church is called his body—like a physical body, it is made up of many parts. And just as each part of a physical body has a different role in doing the body's work and keeping it healthy, each member of the body of Christ has a distinct and necessary responsibility to the whole. It's an honor for the church to be described in a way that so beautifully illustrates its role as Christ's partner in his work on earth.

All of you together are Christ's body, and each of you is a part of it.
1 CORINTHIANS 12:27

Q. WHY IS THE CHURCH CALLED "THE BRIDE OF CHRIST"?

How can a group of so many people be a bride?

A. In the Bible the church is described as the bride of Christ. Jesus referred to himself as "the bridegroom," using this beautiful symbolic term for the relationship between him and his body of believers. Think about it. A bride is loved very much by her groom. They plan a future together and do life together. The term fits, doesn't it?

If you've ever been around someone who is getting married and felt the joy and expectation that a coming wedding brings, it makes even more sense. In Bible times, brides and grooms were kept separated during the preparations leading up to the wedding day. They waited with anticipation and stayed true to each other. Sound familiar? As we wait for Jesus to return, we prepare by learning more about him and living for him. We remain faithful by loving him with our obedience, and our anticipation grows as we wait. What an exciting reunion it will be when the wedding day finally arrives!

"Let us be glad and rejoice. . . . For the time has come for the wedding feast of the Lamb, and his bride has prepared herself. She has been given the finest of pure white linen to wear." For the fine linen represents the good deeds of God's holy people.

REVELATION 19:7-8

Q. DOES A CHURCH REQUIRE A BUILDING?

If there is no building, how do people know where the church is?

A. In our society, we are accustomed to thinking of a church as a building—a brick structure, a little wooden building with a steeple, or even a storefront. But in the Bible, the word translated as *church* never refers to a building. It is always used to describe a group of *people* who are assembled together for a particular purpose.

Is it convenient to have a designated space where Christians can gather? Of course. Is it necessary? Absolutely not. Any time Christians are together—praying, working, serving—they *are* the church, no matter where they gather.

So why did churches come to be known as buildings? At some point, groups of Christians felt the need for a place in which to worship. Perhaps they were thinking of the Temple, a place where the ancient Israelites came to offer sacrifices and where God's presence dwelt. But since the Holy Spirit now lives in the hearts of believers rather than in a physical structure, a church building is not necessary. Believers *are* the church.

- -

Together, we are his house, built on the foundation of the apostles and the prophets. And the cornerstone is Christ Jesus himself. We are carefully joined together in him, becoming a holy temple for the Lord. EPHESIANS 2:20-21

Q. WHAT'S THE DIFFERENCE BETWEEN A CHURCH AND THE CHURCH?

I've heard it both ways. Are they the same thing?

A. When we talk about "going to church," we're usually talking about going to a specific physical location to worship and spend time with other Christians. Even though we know that the church is not a building, we still think of it in terms of a congregation—a particular group of people who know one another and meet together regularly. That's *a* church.

The church is something much bigger and more wonderful. It includes more than an individual congregation in a specific place, more than a denominational organization. *The* church, sometimes called "the church universal," is all Christians everywhere, past and present—united, despite our denominational differences, in our common love for Jesus and our trust in him as Savior.

- -

And his name will be the hope of all the world. MATTHEW 12:21

Q. WHY IS IT IMPORTANT TO GO TO CHURCH?

I'm not sure that church is my thing. Do I have to go to church to be a Christian?

A. Being a Christian means that you have confessed your sins to Jesus and accepted his forgiveness. You can do that on your own, without attending or joining a church. However, Jesus never intended for his followers to be solitary, secret believers. He established the church as an opportunity for people who believe in him to gather together to share life, worship him, and learn about God and his ways.

All of those are good reasons to be part of a church. An even better reason is that Jesus started the church and desires for us to be part of it. If you are a follower of Jesus Christ, you need the church—and the church needs you! Just as your body relies on food and water to function well, your spiritual health relies on teaching, worship, and community to grow. But remember, too, that there are many, many different kinds of churches. If one doesn't seem to fit after you have given it a fair chance, you can always try another.

Just as our bodies have many parts and each part has a special function, so it is with Christ's body. We are many parts of one body, and we all belong to each other. ROMANS 12:4-5

Q. BUT CAN'T I WORSHIP GOD AND PRAY ON MY OWN?

God isn't confined to a building. He's everywhere, right?

A. Of course you can worship when you're by yourself. And you should! You may know of special places that motivate your heart to praise God or appreciate opportunities to pray and study on your own. There's nothing wrong with that. But it doesn't take away your need to be part of a church.

Jesus actually promised his presence wherever groups of two or more believers gather in his name. That's not to say he's not with you as an individual. But something special happens when members of God's family are together in one place.

Your church family will encourage you as you do God's work. They will pray with you and enrich your experience of worship. They will help you learn as you study God's Word together. They will support you during difficult times and hold you accountable if you drift away from God. They will care about you—and you will do the same for them.

Do all churches function this way? Sadly, no. But that's no reason to give up on church. Instead, we are called to participate in making the church everything Jesus meant for it to be.

Let us not neglect our meeting together, as some people do, but encourage one another, especially now that the day of his return is drawing near. HEBREWS 10:25

Q. ISN'T THE CHURCH FULL OF HYPOCRITES?

How can Christians claim to follow God but sometimes be unloving, unkind, and dishonest?

A. The church is made up of people, and all people are sinners. Even those who try to live in obedience to God will fail from time to time. That's not necessarily hypocritical. It's just being human.

Some people, on the other hand, pay lip service to Christian values but don't bother to live in obedience to Jesus Christ. They claim to follow him but still gossip, lie, cheat, and treat others unkindly—all while keeping up the facade of being "good Christians." These people really are hypocrites. And yes, some of them are in the church.

But not everyone in the church is like that. There are many humble, loving, honest Christians who strive to model their lives after Jesus' example. They have pure motives and are committed to bringing glory to God alone. Be on the lookout for them when you attend church, and strive to get to know them.

○ ○ ○ ○ ○ ● ○ ○ ○ ○ ○ ○ ○ ○ ○ ○ ● ○ ● ● ○ ○ ○ ○ ○ ○ ○ ○

Everyone has sinned; we all fall short of God's glorious standard.
ROMANS 3:23

Q. WHY DO CHURCH PEOPLE FIGHT AMONG THEMSELVES?

Aren't Christians supposed to get along with one another?

A. Yes, they are . . . and in a perfect world, they always would. Unfortunately, this world is far from perfect, and Christians are humans who behave selfishly sometimes. But one of the great things about being part of a church body is that members can hold one another accountable. If one person is behaving badly toward someone, ideally a church friend can say, "Hey, it doesn't seem like you are showing Christ's love here."

That's the way Jesus meant for the church to function. From the pastor to the elder board to deacons to congregants, a church should help all believers stay true to living for Jesus by showing love to one another and to those outside the church. There may be disagreements and problems at times, just as there may be in any social setting, but hopefully Christians can handle them in a way that shows God's love and honors him.

○ ○ ○ ● ○ ○ ○ ○ ○ ● ● ● ○ ● ○ ● ○ ○ ○ ○ ● ○ ○ ● ○ ○ ● ○ ○

[Jesus said,] "I am giving you a new commandment: Love each other. Just as I have loved you, you should love each other. Your love for one another will prove to the world that you are my disciples." JOHN 13:34-35

Q. WHY DO CHURCHES ASK FOR CONTRIBUTIONS?

Shouldn't they be more interested in souls than money?

A. The concept of giving to God's work started when the Israelites were instructed to give a tenth of the animals from their flocks and herds, as well as a tenth of their agricultural produce (called a tithe), back to the Lord as a sacrifice and to provide food for the priests. In New Testament times, churches continued this concept by pooling their resources to care for members and further their outreach.

Today, believers are still expected to contribute to God's work. Ministers and missionaries must support their families, while churches and Christian organizations need funds to maintain their ministries. Running a church building and purchasing supplies cost money.

But there's a deeper reason that Christians are asked to give. It's because sharing what we have (with the right attitude) is good for our souls. Giving is an exercise in gratitude—remembering that everything we have is a gift from God in the first place. It teaches us to trust, believing God's promise that when we give, we will be blessed. And it helps us feel part of the wonderful things that God is doing in the world.

You must each decide in your heart how much to give. And don't give reluctantly or in response to pressure. "For God loves a person who gives cheerfully." 2 CORINTHIANS 9:7

42

Q. WHY ARE THERE SO MANY DIFFERENT KINDS OF CHURCHES?

It's really confusing to sort them all out!

A. The church has been around for nearly two thousand years. Not surprisingly, during that time there have been disagreements. Some involved substantial matters of belief, while others were mostly matters of culture, worship style, or political issues. And sadly, some resulted in ugly conflicts that split the church into factions.

The church today is made up of many different denominations—groups of churches with their own core beliefs and methods of worship and teaching. There are Eastern Orthodox and Roman Catholic churches and many varieties of Protestant churches ranging from mainline Lutherans and Methodists to more evangelical Baptists and Pentecostals, plus an array of nondenominational churches.

Are the differences important? Yes and no. The disagreements and variances in practice and theology are real. But if a church recognizes Jesus as Lord and teaches biblical truth, that's what really matters. Instead of arguing, churches should work together to share the message of God's love with everyone. The good news is that many of them do just that!

[Jesus said,] "I pray that they will all be one, just as you and I are one—as you are in me, Father, and I am in you. And may they be in us so that the world will believe you sent me." JOHN 17:21

Q. ARE THERE SOME THINGS __ALL__ CHURCHES DO ALIKE?

What do they have in common?

A. Church traditions and cultures vary widely in style and theology, but they also share a lot of similarities. Here are a few things you'll encounter in almost any church:

- *Music.* Whether they sing hymns or praise songs—whether they have an organ, a rock band, or no instruments at all—most Christians love to raise their voices to God.
- *Prayer.* Christians pray together, with many reciting Jesus' model prayer from Matthew 6:9-13.
- *Bible reading.* Some follow a lectionary—a planned-out sequence of readings—while others choose passages that seem relevant to the day.
- *A spoken message* (often called a sermon or a homily). These range from brief reflections to meaty "teachings."

In addition, almost all churches celebrate Communion on a regular basis—partaking of bread and wine or grape juice as a remembrance of Jesus' death and resurrection—and almost all offer baptism. You'll also find that many churches love to share food and fellowship. You're welcome to join them!

○ ○ ○ ○ ○ ● ○ ○ ○ ○ ○ ○ ○ ○ ● ○ ○ ● ○ ● ● ○ ○ ○ ○ ○ ● ○ ○

Let the message about Christ, in all its richness, fill your lives. Teach and counsel each other with all the wisdom he gives. Sing psalms and hymns and spiritual songs to God with thankful hearts. COLOSSIANS 3:16

Q. WHAT IS BAPTISM?

What does it mean?

A. Baptism is something Jesus commanded before he went back to heaven. It is an outward display of the inward change in your heart.

Churches approach baptism in different ways. In some, people are lowered under the water (a picture of Jesus' death, burial, and resurrection), while in others, water is poured or sprinkled over the head of the person being baptized.

Churches also differ as to *when* a person can be baptized. All baptize adults and older children who make the decision to accept Jesus. But some also baptize infants as a sign of the parents' and the church's commitment to raise them in the Christian faith. These babies will later be "confirmed" when they are old enough to willingly decide that they will follow Jesus.

Whatever the church tradition, baptism is always done "in the name of the Father and the Son and the Holy Spirit" (Matthew 28:19), and all forms of baptism symbolize the washing away of sin and the beginning of a new life in Christ.

* °

You were buried with Christ when you were baptized. And with him you were raised to new life because you trusted the mighty power of God, who raised Christ from the dead.

COLOSSIANS 2:12

Q. WHAT IS COMMUNION?

Why is it so important to Christians?

A. Jesus instituted the model for our modern-day practice of Communion when he shared the Passover meal with his disciples just before he was arrested. Jesus took some bread, thanked God for it, and broke it in pieces, saying, "This is my body, which is given for you." Then he took a cup of wine and told them, "This cup is the new covenant between God and his people—an agreement confirmed with my blood, which is poured out as a sacrifice for you" (Luke 22:20). With these words, Jesus was predicting his own death, which was only hours away. He urged the disciples to remember the meaning of eating the bread and drinking the wine and to repeat it often.

This practice of sharing bread and wine (or grape juice) and remembering Jesus' sacrifice is known by various names today—Communion, the Eucharist, the Lord's Supper—but it is practiced in most Christian denominations. Whether your church celebrates it every week or less often, Communion is a good time to confess your sins, think of Jesus' death and resurrection, and thank him for his amazing love.

- -

Every time you eat this bread and drink this cup, you are announcing the Lord's death until he comes again.

1 CORINTHIANS 11:26

Q. CAN ANYONE PARTICIPATE IN COMMUNION?

What is involved in partaking of the service?

A. Communion is a special time for Christians. The bread and wine represent the sacrifice of Jesus' body and blood. This is a time to remember what he did for us on the cross and give thanks. It is also a time of special togetherness for the family of God gathered in a particular place.

Not surprisingly, different denominations have developed Communion traditions that reflect their distinctive views. Some allow all in attendance, including children, to participate. Others reserve Communion for adult members of the congregation. Participants are often encouraged to observe a short time of private introspection before partaking of the "elements," as the bread and wine are often called. The bread may resemble a loaf, a flat cracker, or a thin wafer, and the wine or grape juice may be served from a common cup or tiny individual ones. Church members may file to the front or pass the elements while seated. If you're unsure of what to do in a particular church, just ask. Church members will be happy to welcome you and explain their particular traditions.

- -

Anyone who eats this bread or drinks this cup of the Lord unworthily is guilty of sinning against the body and blood of the Lord. That is why you should examine yourself before eating the bread and drinking the cup. 1 CORINTHIANS 11:27-28

Q. IS THE SABBATH ON SUNDAY?

Does it matter what day I go to church?

A. Keeping the Sabbath is one of God's original rules for the Israelites and is one of the Ten Commandments. Because God had rested on the seventh day of Creation, his people were commanded to set aside a special day for rest and worship. It was supposed to be different from every other day of the week, dedicated to drawing closer to God.

The ancient Israelites and the Jewish people of Jesus' time observed the Sabbath at the end of the week—on the seventh day. This practice is still followed by observant Jews and some Christian denominations, who begin their Sabbath at sundown on Friday and continue to observe it until sundown on Saturday. Based on the account of Creation in the book of Genesis, the ancient Israelites marked sundown as the start of a new day.

Today, the majority of Christian churches observe the Sabbath on Sunday to honor the tradition of Jesus' resurrection occurring on the first day of the week. But some choose to hold services or take a personal Sabbath on a different day. Ministers who do their work on Sunday, for instance, may set aside another day of the week for quiet, rest, and reflection.

Remember to observe the Sabbath day by keeping it holy.

EXODUS 20:8

Q. WHAT DOES IT MEAN TO OBSERVE THE SABBATH?

Is it all about going to church?

A. The Sabbath was originally given to the Israelites as a gift, a time to rest from work and draw closer to God. By Jesus' time, however, the religious authorities had developed very complicated rules about what people could and could not do on the Sabbath. They even accused Jesus of violating it by healing someone. But Jesus argued that they were missing the whole point of the Sabbath—which was to meet people's needs! Today, we can honor the Sabbath—without missing the point—by focusing on a few very basic principles:

- The Sabbath should be different and special—set aside for nurturing our relationship with God.
- It should involve prayer and worship, ideally with other believers.
- It should be restful, allowing us to slow down and recharge our batteries.

Most Christians do go to church on the Sabbath. Some also share a special meal with their families or other believers, enjoy a nap, or take a walk. Whatever helps you rest and draw closer to God and those you love—without judging others—is an appropriate way to enjoy God's Sabbath gift.

The Sabbath was made to meet the needs of people, and not people to meet the requirements of the Sabbath. MARK 2:27

Q. WHAT IS THE PURPOSE OF SUNDAY SCHOOL?

Don't kids get enough school during the week?

A. Sunday school was started in the nineteenth century for children who had to work in factories during the week. These early Sunday schools not only served to educate children about the Bible but also helped them with reading and other basic skills. Today, however, the emphasis in most Sunday schools (and other institutions for Christian education) is on teaching about God and the Bible.

The Bible doesn't mention Sunday school, of course, but it does stress that each successive generation must be taught about God's principles, commandments, and character qualities. This can and should be done at home, but Sunday school is another important resource for bringing up children in the Christian faith. And Christian education doesn't stop once we become adults. We never outgrow the need to keep on learning and growing as Christians.

○ ○ ○ ○ ○ ● ○ ○ ○ ● ○ ○ ○ ○ ○ ○ ● ● ● ○ ○ ○ ○ ○ ● ○ ○ ○

We . . . will tell the next generation about the glorious deeds of the LORD, about his power and his mighty wonders. . . . So each generation should set its hope anew on God.   PSALM 78:4, 7

Q. WHAT'S THE DIFFERENCE BETWEEN PASTORS, PREACHERS, MINISTERS, AND PRIESTS?

Are they all just names for the leader of a church?

A. Each of these terms is used to describe professional church leaders—those who have been licensed or ordained (inducted into service in a special ritual) and who receive a salary or some other kind of support. Such leaders are often called "clergy." But each title has a distinctive meaning as well.

Pastor means "shepherd," and that's what pastors are. They lead and guide the people in their churches. In many churches, a pastor is the one in charge.

A *preacher* is someone who delivers a message or sermon. Most pastors are preachers, but not every preacher is a pastor.

The same is true of *ministers*. To minister means to serve, and ministers serve God and others in many ways—including leading churches.

Priests are those who conduct the rituals observed in Catholic, Orthodox, and Anglican congregations. They may also be called pastors or ministers in some circumstances.

If you are unsure what to call a member of the clergy, you can always ask. They'll be glad to let you know.

o o o o o o o o o o o o o o o o o o o o o o o o o o o

I will give you shepherds after my own heart, who will guide you with knowledge and understanding. JEREMIAH 3:15

Q. WHAT ARE DEACONS?

Are they ministers too?

A. Deacons have served an important role in the church since New Testament times. Almost all churches have them, though the specific "job description" differs according to the denomination. In Catholic, Orthodox, and Anglican churches, deacons are ordained as clergy, and most go on to become priests. In other churches, deacons are regular members of the congregation.

Deacons fulfill many roles in a church. Some focus on the worship aspect of congregational services and church life. Others perform practical functions like making repairs or helping with outreach programs. But the defining characteristic of a deacon is *service.* The word *deacon* originally meant *servant* in the sense of waiting tables—because that's what the first deacons did! They were appointed to help distribute food and take care of the needy so the apostles could be free to preach the gospel. Stephen, one of the first deacons and the first Christian martyr, was stoned to death because he was an outspoken follower of Jesus.

Those who do well as deacons will be rewarded with respect from others and will have increased confidence in their faith in Christ Jesus. 1 TIMOTHY 3:13

Q. WHAT ARE ELDERS?

Are they basically just the older people in a church?

A. The term *elder* does refer to an older person, but in the New Testament it is used more specifically to refer to a wise person who holds a position of responsibility in the church. The Bible talks a lot about elders, so clearly their leadership was vital to the growing church. Their purpose was to mediate disputes, set a good example, teach, and pray for the sick. Essentially they were the leaders of the local church.

Today the term *elder* is used many ways. In some denominations it is an official title for someone who shares responsibility in leading the church. In others the term describes an older member of a church whom everyone recognizes as wise and experienced. Sometimes it's used synonymously with *minister* or *deacon*. Whatever the official responsibility, the qualifications spelled out in the Bible still apply: Elders must be experienced Christians who are recognized as moral and upright, having their own lives in order and the ability to effectively teach others biblical truth.

Guard yourselves and God's people. Feed and shepherd God's flock—his church, purchased with his own blood—over which the Holy Spirit has appointed you as leaders. ACTS 20:28

Q. WHAT IS A MINISTRY?

What exactly does that word mean? Do I have to be a minister to have a ministry?

A. A ministry is a particular form of service to God and others. It is common to refer to pastors and priests as ministers, but ministry is not limited to these professionals. There are many different kinds of ministries, and some are associated with churches and others function as separate organizations.

You might know of Christians who teach Sunday school or are involved with children's Bible clubs. Those are examples of ministries. So are Bible study groups and soup kitchens and winter clothing drives. Ministries are usually organized to serve people who have a common need—for food, clothing, or a chance to hear about God's love. In addition to providing helpful services, ministries give God's people opportunities to grow personally as they learn new skills and share their faith with others.

○ ○ ○ ○ ○ ● ○ ○ ○ ○ ○ ● ○ ○ ○ ○ ○ ● ○ ○ ● ● ○ ○ ○ ○ ○ ● ○ ○

Just as you accepted Christ Jesus as your Lord, you must continue to follow him. Let your roots grow down into him, and let your lives be built on him. Then your faith will grow strong in the truth you were taught, and you will overflow with thankfulness.

COLOSSIANS 2:6-7

Q. WHAT ARE SPIRITUAL GIFTS?

Does everyone have them? Can I choose which one I want?

A. Spiritual gifts are abilities or talents that God gives his children to equip them for the work he has planned for them. You do not choose your own gift—the Holy Spirit chooses it for you!

Scripture provides three different lists of spiritual gifts—in Romans 12:6-8, 1 Corinthians 12:4-11, and 1 Corinthians 12:27-28. The gifts listed include prophecy, serving, teaching, encouraging, giving, leadership, wisdom, knowledge, faith, healing, miracles, showing mercy, helping others, and the ability to speak in foreign languages—or even a heavenly language—and also to interpret what's being spoken.

How do you know what your special gift is? This may take some time and discernment. Think about what forms of ministry just feel right. What do you especially enjoy? What skills or characteristics do others recognize in you and seem blessed by? Ask the Holy Spirit to help you recognize and use your gift. And don't be afraid to take advantage of new ministry opportunities. Everything you try might give you new insight into how God wants to use you—and none of your work for him will be wasted.

○ ○ ○ ○ ○ ○ ○ ○ ○ ○ ● ○ ○ ○ ○ ○ ○ ○ ○ ○ ○ ○ ○ ○ ○

God has given each of you a gift from his great variety of spiritual gifts. Use them well to serve one another. 1 PETER 4:10

Q. WHAT IS EVANGELISM?

Is it the same thing as ministry?

A. When you have good news, don't you want to share it with others? That's basically what the word *evangelism* means—it comes from the Greek word for *gospel* or *good news*. Evangelism is the process of sharing the good news of Jesus' life, death, and resurrection with others for the purpose of leading them to faith in him. Professional preachers and missionaries are sometimes called evangelists because they are "specialists" in sharing the gospel. But evangelism is really for every Christian because Jesus gave all believers the responsibility of sharing God's love.

Christians approach evangelism in different ways, using their own strengths and abilities. Evangelism can happen on a platform at a conference, over coffee or a meal shared between friends, or on a park bench with a new acquaintance. It can happen in the context of ministry (serving others), but it can happen in the midst of ordinary life as well. Each of us should share about Jesus in a way that feels comfortable. Our news is too good to keep quiet about!

- -

We are Christ's ambassadors; God is making his appeal through us. We speak for Christ when we plead, "Come back to God!" 2 CORINTHIANS 5:20

Q. WHAT IS "THE GREAT COMMISSION"?

Who is being commissioned? Is it for everyone?

A. The great commission is a command Jesus gave to his followers before he ascended to heaven. It is a simple command, but it outlines what Jesus expects all his disciples to do. Wherever we go and whatever we do—even in our normal, everyday lives—we should be sharing our faith. This job is not just for pastors or missionaries, and there's more to it than presenting information. In fact, it's vital that we "show" our faith as well as "tell" about it—living lives that reveal God's love.

All of this involves not only bringing people to Jesus for his saving forgiveness but also "making disciples," which means teaching people how to love God and nurture their faith so it grows stronger and deeper. This, too, is accomplished both by words and by modeling God's love with our actions.

- -

[Jesus said,] "Go and make disciples of all the nations, baptizing them in the name of the Father and the Son and the Holy Spirit. Teach these new disciples to obey all the commands I have given you." MATTHEW 28:19-20

Q. WHY DOES THE CHURCH SEND OUT MISSIONARIES?

Isn't it hard for people to move away from their families and go to unfamiliar places? Why do they do it?

A. God wants all people—everywhere—to hear about his wonderful love. But some people in the remote places of the world don't even have a Bible in their language. And plenty of people who have Bibles in their language still have never heard about Jesus and are not likely to visit a church. That's why we need missionaries—people who leave home to share God's love, either in their own country or abroad.

Some missionaries translate the Bible into other languages. Others learn languages native to the land where they're serving so they can teach the Bible to willing disciples. It's also common for missionaries to start churches, serve as doctors and nurses, and participate in humanitarian work. Life can be rewarding as they see evidence of God's hand in their efforts, but it can also be tiring and even dangerous.

Those who become missionaries are doing what God has called them to do. Is it hard to leave their families? Most certainly, yes. But they're motivated by a deep desire to obey God and help others encounter God's amazing love.

The Good News about [God's] Kingdom will be preached throughout the whole world, so that all nations will hear it.
MATTHEW 24:14

Q. WHAT IS "CHURCH PLANTING"?

That's a strange term. Does it symbolically parallel planting a field or a garden?

A. "Church planting" *is* kind of a strange term, but it makes sense when you think about it. When you plant flowers or vegetables, you put a seed in the ground, water it, let the sun shine on it, and wait for it to grow. Church planting works in a similar way.

New churches are planted because an established church or ministry notices an area that doesn't have any (or many) churches. So a few families or individuals will start holding church services in that area. To get the word out, they advertise and personally extend invitations to visit their new church. Relationships built, love shared, and plenty of prayer are the "watering" and "sunshine" that cause a church plant to grow. It may take considerable time and patience, but with God's blessings a new church will begin to grow.

[Paul wrote,] My ambition has always been to preach the Good News where the name of Christ has never been heard, rather than where a church has already been started by someone else. I have been following the plan spoken of in the Scriptures ... "Those who have never been told about him will see, and those who have never heard of him will understand." ROMANS 15:20-21

Q. DOES GOD HAVE WORK FOR EVERYONE TO DO?

I'm just an ordinary person. What can I do?

A. Maybe you're not a trained Bible scholar, a pastor, a deacon, or a missionary. What kind of ministry can an "ordinary person" have?

- You can reach out to people you meet and befriend them.
- You can invite friends to church or a Bible study.
- You can share in simple words what your faith means to you.
- You can pray—for the church and its leaders, for your family and friends, for people you meet.
- You can look for jobs at church that need to get done—anything from teaching the kids to serving on a committee to helping with the newsletter—and pitch in.
- You can use your spiritual gifts and talents creatively to support God's work. (If you don't know what your gifts are, talk to your pastor or someone in your church who can help you discover them.)
- You can do your very best to obey God and live a life that pleases him. Don't underestimate the influence that comes from living lovingly and obediently.

Be an example to all believers in what you say, in the way you live, in your love, your faith, and your purity. 1 TIMOTHY 4:12

Q. HOW CAN I FIND THE RIGHT CHURCH FOR ME?

There are so many kinds. I don't even know where to start.

A. It's important to seek out a church where the people love Jesus and take the Bible seriously, where you are encouraged and your spirit is nourished. Beyond that, finding the right church is mostly a matter of what you feel "fits." However, seeking the right church should be more like looking for a relationship where you are challenged to grow than going through a cafeteria line to pick only the items you want. Here are some suggestions:

- Pray about it! If you ask God to lead you, he will.
- Think about what you like, but keep an open mind. God might have other ideas!
- Do a little research. Most churches have helpful websites. Ask churchgoing friends where they go and why.
- Visit churches that interest you. Read the leaflet, participate in the service, and stay afterward for coffee and fellowship.
- Give each church you visit a chance. Even if you decide not to stay, you can benefit from learning about different church traditions.

So now you . . . are no longer strangers and foreigners. You are citizens along with all of God's holy people. You are members of God's family. EPHESIANS 2:19

Part 3

QUESTIONS AND ANSWERS ABOUT YOUR FUTURE AND THE FUTURE OF THE WORLD

Q. WHAT HAPPENS TO US AFTER WE DIE?

Does the Bible teach that there's life after death?

A. The Bible makes it very clear that physical death is not the end. There is indeed life after death, and it lasts forever. Whether that is good news or not depends on the choices a person makes *before* death.

The night before Jesus died on the cross, he told his disciples he was going away to prepare a heavenly home for them. The Bible describes this heaven as a beautiful place where there will be no more sadness—only joy and praise for God.

There is also an afterlife for people who do not accept Jesus, but that life won't be so wonderful. They will spend eternity in the place where Satan is, separated from God and his love. It's known by various names like the *lake of fire*, *hades*, and *hell*. The Bible describes it as a painful place filled with grief, sorrow, anger, and pain.

This is a serious matter, which is why we must tell others about God's love and his desire to spend eternity with them.

[Jesus said,] "Don't let your hearts be troubled. Trust in God, and trust also in me. There is more than enough room in my Father's home. If this were not so, would I have told you that I am going to prepare a place for you?" JOHN 14:1-2

Q. WHAT IS THE BOOK OF LIFE?

Does God keep an actual record of people he likes? How do I make sure my name is included?

A. The Book of Life is mentioned several times in the Bible—a few times in the Psalms, once in Paul's letters, and multiple times in the book of Revelation. These passages do seem to indicate that if your name is not listed in this book, you will not be welcomed into God's heaven and will spend eternity apart from him. The names in the book aren't simply people God likes, but those who have trusted Jesus as Savior.

How can you be sure that your name is in the Book of Life? Ask him to be your Savior—confess your sins to Jesus and believe he has forgiven you. Commit to obey his commands and live for him. When you do that, your name is written in the Book of Life for good. It will not be erased just because you commit a sin or even give up on God for a while. You will spend eternity with Jesus. That's Good News!

All who are victorious will be clothed in white. I will never erase their names from the Book of Life, but I will announce before my Father and his angels that they are mine. REVELATION 3:5

Q. WHERE IS HEAVEN?

Is it high up in the sky?

A. There are three heavens mentioned in the Bible. The first heaven is where the birds fly and the clouds float—what we call the sky or the atmosphere. The second heaven is what we call outer space—where the sun, moon, and stars are. The third heaven is where God is, and no one knows exactly where that is. Some descriptions are given in the Bible, especially in the book of Revelation, but heaven's location isn't specified.

Is the third heaven thousands and thousands of miles above us? Perhaps. Is it all around us but invisible? Maybe. Is it in another dimension entirely? We don't know. What we do know is that heaven is a real place and that it is *huge*.

Actually, the exact location of heaven isn't important. What *is* important is that God is in heaven and one day those who love him will be also.

○ ○ ○ ○ ○ ● ○ ○ ○ ● ○ ○ ○ ○ ○ ○ ● ○ ● ● ○○ ○ ○ ○ ● ○ ○ ○

Look, the highest heavens and the earth and everything in it all belong to the LORD your God.   DEUTERONOMY 10:14

Q. DO WE GO TO HEAVEN (OR HELL) IMMEDIATELY AFTER WE DIE?

Or must we wait until Jesus comes back to earth?

A. Committed Christians hold different opinions about this. Some believe that Jesus' followers go directly to heaven after they die and that those who have rejected Jesus go directly to hell. Others believe there is a delay between the moment of death and the promised judgment when Jesus returns. Perhaps, they reason, we stay in some kind of suspended state where we are not aware of time.

Much of what happens after death remains a mystery to those of us still living. But Scripture makes several things clear: First, we will still be ourselves after we die. Second, the souls of believers who have died are present with the Lord. Their physical bodies will be resurrected, and they will spend eternity with him. And third, Christians have no reason at all to fear death.

∘ ∘

Now we see things imperfectly, like puzzling reflections in a mirror, but then we will see everything with perfect clarity. All that I know now is partial and incomplete, but then I will know everything completely, just as God now knows me completely.

1 CORINTHIANS 13:12

Q. WHAT WILL I DO IN HEAVEN?

Will I just praise God all the time?

A. From an earthly perspective, it might seem like praising God forever and ever would get boring. But our minds cannot comprehend how overwhelming (in a good way) it will be to actually be in his presence. Eternity may not be long enough to praise him!

But there is another thing to consider about living in heaven: God promises that it will be a wonderful experience. It's quite likely that the talents, gifts, and interests God has given us here on earth—the things we love doing—will also be a major part of our experience in heaven. How wonderful would it be to enjoy those interests without the limitations we now face in a world steeped in sin?

We can be sure that whatever we spend our time doing, it will be pleasant and filled with joy . . . and praise for God!

- -

No eye has seen, no ear has heard, and no mind has imagined what God has prepared for those who love him.

1 CORINTHIANS 2:9

Q. WILL I HAVE MY SAME BODY IN HEAVEN?

Will everyone look the same as when they were alive on earth?

A. The Bible tells us we will have bodies of some kind in heaven. Job said, "In my body I will see God!" (Job 19:26). In the book of Revelation, John writes about a celebration banquet that takes place in heaven, so it seems that we'll be able to eat.

However, we won't have the exact same bodies that we have here on earth. Our current bodies have been tainted by sin and will eventually die. In order to live eternally in heaven, our bodies must be changed.

Scripture tells us that when Jesus returns, God will resurrect our bodies so they are like Jesus' resurrected body. What exactly they will be like is a mystery, but we know that whatever God has for us in heaven will be amazing!

— —

Our physical bodies cannot inherit the Kingdom of God. These dying bodies cannot inherit what will last forever. . . . Our dying bodies must be transformed into bodies that will never die; our mortal bodies must be transformed into immortal bodies.

1 CORINTHIANS 15:50, 53

Q. WILL I KNOW MY FRIENDS AND FAMILY IN HEAVEN?

I want to see Jesus, but I also want to see loved ones who have gone before me.

A. There are a few biblical references to people who saw and recognized others who had died: The prophet Samuel, who had died not long before, communicated to King Saul in a vision (1 Samuel 28). Jesus told a parable about a beggar and a rich man who knew each other on earth; both men died, and the rich man went to hell, while the beggar did not. In his torment, the rich man looked up and saw the beggar enjoying his new life (Luke 16:19-31). And when the long-dead Moses and Elijah appeared to Jesus and some of his disciples on a mountain, they were instantly recognized (Matthew 17:1-9).

So it seems possible that those who were acquainted on earth will recognize each other in heaven. Either way, Jesus will be the supreme focus of heaven. Even if we reunite with loved ones, our joy will be in praising him together.

We want you to know what will happen to the believers who have died so you will not grieve like people who have no hope. For . . . when Jesus returns, God will bring back with him the believers who have died. . . . Then we will be with the Lord forever.

1 THESSALONIANS 4:13-14, 17

Q. WILL I FEEL SORROW IN HEAVEN?

Won't we feel sad if people we love aren't there?

A. It's hard to imagine not being sad about loved ones who aren't in heaven, but heaven will be so joyfully overwhelming with the presence of God that nothing else will occupy our minds. We will be so amazed at the beauty and holiness of God the Father and Jesus his Son that we'll desire to worship them continually.

With all of our attention on them, it's unlikely we will notice that some of those we love aren't there. Perhaps God will help us to focus on who *is* there instead of who isn't. Scripture does tell us clearly that there will be no sadness or crying in heaven, so we can expect only to be filled with joy when we are in his presence.

He will wipe every tear from their eyes, and there will be no more death or sorrow or crying or pain. All these things are gone forever. REVELATION 21:4

Q. DOES BEING RAISED AS A CHRISTIAN MEAN THAT I WILL GO TO HEAVEN?

Will God let me in if my parents are there?

A. If you grew up in a Christian family with parents who loved God, you have been blessed. Parents who model faithful Christian lives offer their children a good understanding of what it takes to please God. But is that enough to guarantee you will go to heaven when you die?

While some may wish it were that simple, the Bible makes it very clear that choosing to follow Jesus is a personal decision. Having Christian parents—or other Christian role models in your life—is a wonderful heritage, but it has nothing to do with whether or not you will inherit eternal life. It is a choice you must make for yourself.

o o o o o ● o o o o o o o o o o ● ● ● o o o o o ● o o

Anyone who believes in God's Son has eternal life. Anyone who doesn't obey the Son will never experience eternal life but remains under God's angry judgment. JOHN 3:36

Q. IS LIVING A GOOD LIFE ENOUGH TO GUARANTEE I'LL GO TO HEAVEN?

I try to do the right thing and be a good person. Isn't that enough to get me into heaven?

A. Sometimes people think that as long as they are honest, loving, and helpful toward others, they'll automatically go to heaven when they die. Those are certainly good qualities, and Jesus himself urged people to behave that way. But he also said there is only one way into heaven—through him.

Everyone decides for herself or himself whether to believe in God and accept the forgiveness and salvation that Jesus offers. No matter how good a person is, choosing not to accept this gift means he or she will spend eternity apart from God and the beauty and joy of heaven. The Bible admonishes us, "What makes us think we can escape if we ignore this great salvation?" (Hebrews 2:3). How very true—it would be a terrible tragedy to not accept the wonderful gift that Jesus offers.

Jesus told [Thomas], "I am the way, the truth, and the life. No one can come to the Father except through me." JOHN 14:6

Q. DO BABIES WHO DIE GO TO HEAVEN?

Are babies and young children allowed in heaven if they die without asking Jesus to forgive their sins?

A. The Bible teaches that only those who confess their sins and accept Jesus' forgiveness will be permitted in heaven. But are babies and children excluded even though they aren't old enough to know that?

Most Bible scholars agree there is an age when people can sense they are sinners in need of a Savior. It's called the age of accountability, and it may be different for different people—God knows when a person is mature enough to grasp this.

The consensus among these scholars is that if babies and children die before reaching the age of accountability, God welcomes them into heaven. He would not reject someone who can't even understand that he or she needs salvation. God is righteous and just in all of his ways, and he wants everyone to have the chance to know him.

The teachers of religious law saw these wonderful miracles and heard even the children in the Temple shouting, "Praise God for the Son of David." But the leaders were indignant. They asked Jesus, "Do you hear what these children are saying?" "Yes," Jesus replied. "Haven't you ever read the Scriptures? For they say, 'You have taught children and infants to give you praise.'"

MATTHEW 21:15-16

Q. WHAT ABOUT ADULTS WHO HAVE NEVER HEARD OF JESUS?

Is there any way for them to go to heaven?

A. This is a tough question, and many thoughtful Christians have wrestled with this—and come up with different answers.

One possible way to think about this question is to view it through the argument the apostle Paul makes that there are many ways people can recognize God (see Romans 1). One way is through the amazing beauty and complexity of creation, which points toward a Creator. Another way is through their own hearts—a built-in sense that God exists and a basic idea of right and wrong. This means that people who have not heard about Jesus still have the capacity to recognize and respond to God. For those who do, it is reasonable to assume that our just and loving God will make a way for them be saved.

Does that negate our call to share the Good News about Jesus? Absolutely not. The way God makes for someone to be redeemed just might be through you or me!

Even Gentiles, who do not have God's written law, show that they know his law when they instinctively obey it, even without having heard it. They demonstrate that God's law is written in their hearts, for their own conscience and thoughts either accuse them or tell them they are doing right. ROMANS 2:14-15

Q. DO ANIMALS GO TO HEAVEN?

It just won't feel like heaven without my special pet.

A. Pets bring us so much joy, don't they? They give us comfort and companionship. For many of us, they are part of the family. But will they be in heaven with us?

We do know from several Bible passages that there will be animals of various kinds in heaven, but we do not know for certain that our beloved pets will be there. The Bible doesn't specifically address this question. However, some theologians view it like this: If heaven would not seem like heaven for us without our pets, then it's possible that God, in his great love for us, might make a way for them to be there.

○ ○ ○ ○ ● ○ ○ ○ ○ ○ ○ ○ ● ○ ○ ○ ● ● ● ○ ○ ○ ○ ○ ○ ● ○ ○

In that day the wolf and the lamb will live together; the leopard will lie down with the baby goat. The calf and the yearling will be safe with the lion.... The cow will graze near the bear. The cub and the calf will lie down together. The lion will eat hay like a cow.... Nothing will hurt or destroy in all my holy mountain, for as the waters fill the sea, so the earth will be filled with people who know the Lord. ISAIAH 11:6-7, 9

74

Q. DOES IT HURT TO DIE?

I know that after I die I will go to heaven, so I'm not afraid of life after death. But the process of dying scares me. What will it be like?

A. The question of whether it will hurt to die depends on what causes death. It's possible that the experience could be quick and painless—for example, passing away in your sleep. If you are badly injured in an accident, there could likely be pain involved. Or if your body is filled with cancer, the months and days leading up to death might be painful.

But there is no reason to believe that it will hurt when your spirit leaves your body and goes to be with God. We can be assured from what we read in Scripture that when our spirits leave our bodies, they are immediately present with the Lord. Just know that God will never leave you alone, no matter what you're going through.

○ ○ ○ ○ ○ ○ ○ ○ ● ● ○ ○ ○ ○ ○ ○ ○ ○ ● ○ ○ ○ ● ○ ○

We know that when this earthly tent we live in is taken down (that is, when we die and leave this earthly body), we will have a house in heaven, an eternal body made for us by God. . . . We want to put on our new bodies so that these dying bodies will be swallowed up by life. God himself has prepared us for this.

2 CORINTHIANS 5:1, 4-5

Q. IS IT SCARY TO GO TO HEAVEN?

How will I know what to do and where to go?

A. If we look at God's heart as revealed in Scripture, we can feel pretty confident about the answers to these questions. First, God assures us of his love over and over again in the Bible. Because of his love, we who have been redeemed by Jesus can rest securely, knowing that from the moment our souls leave our bodies, he will be with us.

Second, heaven is a reward for believers. Jesus has been getting our heavenly homes ready for us for two thousand years, so they're going to be awesome! Some people even believe that God sends our loved ones who are already in heaven to meet us. If that's true, then we can expect a happy reunion right away. Even better, we will have the most amazing experience of simply being with Jesus. So although going to heaven will be different from anything we have known, it won't be frightening. It will be wonderful!

--- --

We are always confident, even though we know that as long as we live in these bodies we are not at home with the Lord. For we live by believing and not by seeing.... So whether we are here in this body or away from this body, our goal is to please him.

2 CORINTHIANS 5:6-7, 9

Q. WHAT WILL HEAVEN LOOK LIKE?

Will everyone be floating around on clouds?

A. It's true that when people think of heaven, they often picture a sky full of winged angels lazing around on fluffy clouds and playing harps. But there's nothing really biblical about that image.

John, who wrote the book of Revelation, got to peek inside heaven for a bit, and he describes a beautiful city surrounded by a great wall that has three gates on each side. The wall is made of sparkling gemstone, and the city and its streets are constructed of pure gold. The foundation stones are inlaid with precious stones, and the twelve gates are made of pearls. The city is so bright with the glory of God that no lights are needed. Down the main street, flowing from the throne of God, is a sparkling river with a fruitful tree on each side. Their leaves will be used as medicine to heal the nations.

It is hard to even imagine how beautiful this heavenly city will be—and God wants us there! All those who have come to Jesus for salvation will be welcomed.

- -

Nothing evil will be allowed to enter, nor anyone who practices shameful idolatry and dishonesty—but only those whose names are written in the Lamb's [Jesus Christ's] Book of Life.

REVELATION 21:27

Q. WILL I TURN INTO AN ANGEL WHEN I GO TO HEAVEN?

Are angels just the souls of people who have died?

A. When someone dies, you may hear people say something like "Heaven has gained a new angel." But this concept isn't found in the Bible. God created angels for one purpose and humans for another. They are different! Angels have never been human, and human souls do not become angels. When we go to heaven, we will be changed to be like Jesus, but we will still be ourselves.

Angels are spiritual beings who existed before humans. They are intelligent and powerful beings who often serve as God's messengers or his agents. Scripture also describes instances where angels are praising God around his throne.

We humans were made to be "a little lower than the angels," but we were made in God's image and given our own set of privileges and responsibilities. And like the angels, our primary purpose is to worship God and give him glory.

What are mere mortals that you should think about them, or a son of man that you should care for him? Yet for a little while you made them a little lower than the angels and crowned them with glory and honor. You gave them authority over all things. HEBREWS 2:6-8

Q. CAN I GO TO HEAVEN EVEN IF I SIN?

I try to stop sinning, but sometimes I fail. Will God keep me out of heaven?

A. If God kept every sinner out of heaven, then heaven would be pretty empty—because we all sin. God knows it's impossible for us to stop sinning completely, so instead he graciously examines our hearts to discern our truest desires. He knows when we are doing our best to live for him, and he credits us for those good intentions.

Learning to live for God is a journey. The longer we know God, the more we learn about obeying him. And we don't have to be on this journey alone—God helps. From the minute we decide to follow Jesus, God begins working in our hearts and growing us to be more like him.

We still sin sometimes, but we have a remedy. When we confess our wrongdoings and ask God to forgive us, he gives us a fresh start. And as many times as we sincerely ask, he graciously forgives—and forgiven sin will not keep anyone out of heaven.

I am certain that God, who began the good work within you, will continue his work until it is finally finished on the day when Christ Jesus returns. PHILIPPIANS 1:6

Q. IS GOD GLAD THAT I AM COMING TO HEAVEN?

I'm just one person and not even very important. Does God really care if I come to heaven?

A. Billions of people have lived on earth since time began. It's hard to believe that God would notice or care if one specific person comes to his heaven. But as amazing as it seems, God does care! Bible verses like John 3:16 explain that God loves the whole world, but other verses make it clear that he also loves each individual. He wants a relationship with everyone, and he would love to welcome them into his home.

A verse in the book of Luke tells us there is great rejoicing in heaven when one person decides to stop sinning and turns to God. If God and the angels rejoice when you decide to follow Jesus, don't you think God will be waiting for you at heaven's door, thrilled that *you* are finally there?

○ ○ ○ ○ ○ ● ○ ○ ● ○ ○ ○ ○ ○ ○ ● ○ ○ ● ● ● ○ ○ ○ ○ ○ ○ ○ ● ○ ○

There is joy in the presence of God's angels when even one sinner repents. LUKE 15:10

Q. CAN PEOPLE WHO ARE ALREADY IN HEAVEN SEE WHAT WE'RE DOING ON EARTH?

Do my loved ones who have died know what my life is like?

A. The Bible teaches that people in heaven can indeed see some things that are happening on earth. Hebrews 12:1 says that we are surrounded by "a huge crowd of witnesses" in heaven, so it is reasonable to assume they can see how we're progressing in our spiritual growth.

But can our loved ones in heaven see everything we do? Do they know when we help a homeless person or refrain from gossiping about a friend? We simply don't know. What we do know is that heaven is a place of joy and pleasure, so we can hope they're able to glimpse into the lives of people they love on earth. If not, when we get to heaven, we will have a lot to share with them about our lives on earth since they left!

° ° ° ° ° ° ° ° ° • ° ° ° ° ° ° ° ° ° • ° ° ° ° ° °

Since we are surrounded by such a huge crowd of witnesses to the life of faith, let us strip off every weight that slows us down, especially the sin that so easily trips us up. And let us run with endurance the race God has set before us. We do this by keeping our eyes on Jesus, the champion who initiates and perfects our faith. HEBREWS 12:1-2

Q. WHAT DOES IT MEAN TO "STORE UP TREASURE" IN HEAVEN?

Is heaven like a bank? What kind of treasure can I put there?

A. Jesus told his followers to "store up treasure" in heaven by giving to needy people, and he followed that command with "Wherever your treasure is, there the desires of your heart will also be."

Why did Jesus say these things? Storing up treasures in heaven means we value what is close to God's heart more than the things of earth. We pay more attention to God's commands than to other people's opinions. We treasure our relationships with Jesus and others more than we do our material possessions. We put more energy into obeying God and serving others than making a name for ourselves or stockpiling money.

In short, laying up treasure in heaven means investing our lives in what will last forever—the eternal values of heaven—instead of wasting our time and energy on what cannot last.

Sell your possessions and give to those in need. This will store up treasure for you in heaven! And the purses of heaven never get old or develop holes. Your treasure will be safe; no thief can steal it and no moth can destroy it. Wherever your treasure is, there the desires of your heart will also be.   LUKE 12:33-34

Q. WHY SHOULD I SPEND TIME THINKING ABOUT HEAVEN?

Shouldn't I focus on what's happening here and now?

A. The afterlife may seem like a long way off, so why should you spend time thinking about it? One reason is that if you belong to Jesus, heaven will one day be your home—forever. Jesus has been getting a place ready for you there, so it's wise to learn as much about it as you can.

A second reason is that if heaven fills your thoughts, you will live in a way that prepares you for it. Obeying God, loving others, and studying the Bible will become your primary concerns as you follow Jesus' command to store up treasure in heaven. It's a wonderful thing to anticipate such a great reward!

Think about the things of heaven, not the things of earth.

COLOSSIANS 3:2

Q. WHAT IS "THE KINGDOM OF HEAVEN"?

Is it any different from heaven?

A. Jesus used "the Kingdom of Heaven" interchangeably with "the Kingdom of God." He wasn't referring just to heaven, and he wasn't naming a place on earth either. He was speaking of a spiritual reality.

Both of these terms refer to all that God rules over and to the family of those who have accepted the forgiveness and new life that Jesus offers. The Kingdom is eternal, just as God is, and its dominion is present within the souls of all Christians. When we give our lives to Jesus, we become citizens of the Kingdom of God and the Kingdom of Heaven. God is our glorious King, and we will praise him and enjoy him forever!

○ ○ ○ ○ ○ ● ○ ○ ○ ○ ○ ○ ○ ○ ● ○ ○ ● ● ● ○ ○ ○ ○ ● ○ ○

One day the Pharisees asked Jesus, "When will the Kingdom of God come?" Jesus replied, "The Kingdom of God can't be detected by visible signs. You won't be able to say, 'Here it is!' or 'It's over there!' For the Kingdom of God is already among you."

LUKE 17:20-21

Q. WHY DO PEOPLE SAY THE KINGDOM OF GOD IS "NOW BUT NOT YET"?

Can we experience it in our lives now, or do we have to wait until Jesus comes back?

A. The answer to both questions is . . . yes!

The Kingdom of God began when God created the earth and all that is in it. He has always been the rightful ruler of everything, although the rebel Satan assumed temporary jurisdiction over this corrupt and sinful world. But when Jesus died and was resurrected, a whole new dynamic was put in place. He became our once-for-all-time sin sacrifice. After Jesus ascended to heaven, the Holy Spirit came to live in the hearts of his followers, connecting them directly to God's wisdom, guidance, peace, and comfort. When someone becomes a member of God's family and receives the Holy Spirit, that person brings an aspect of God's heart into the world—and the influence of his Kingdom grows!

Since God's Kingdom encompasses all of creation and all believers, it is definitely in place right now. The blessings of being a part of his Kingdom will be realized even more fully after Jesus returns. Then the glory of God and heaven will be shared by all of his children. It hasn't happened yet, but it will!

° °

How great are his signs, how powerful his wonders! His kingdom will last forever, his rule through all generations. DANIEL 4:3

Q. IS HELL A REAL PLACE?

Or is it just a place someone made up to scare us?

A. According to the Bible, hell is just as real as heaven is. It's the place where the souls of people who do not accept Jesus as their Lord and Savior are sent after their bodies die. All people sin, and the built-in consequences of sin are death and separation from God. But Jesus forgives those who believe he gave his life to take the punishment for all the ways they've violated God's laws. Because Jesus has taken away their sins, they are allowed to enter heaven.

Scripture describes hell as a place of torment that lasts forever. It's sometimes called a lake of fire. The people who go to hell will finally recognize that Jesus is God and that he died for their sins, but it will be too late for them to receive his forgiveness. They will spend eternity apart from him.

- -

Then the King will turn to those on the left and say, "Away with you, you cursed ones, into the eternal fire prepared for the devil and his demons." MATTHEW 25:41

Q. WHY WOULD GOD SEND PEOPLE TO HELL?

Isn't he supposed to be all about love?

A. God doesn't want anyone to go to hell. He wouldn't have sent his only Son to earth to die for humanity's sin if he didn't wish that all people would believe in him and accept his gift of salvation. God loves human beings, each and every one.

However, God made it quite clear that the only way to be welcomed into heaven is to believe in Jesus and receive him as your Savior. When you do that, Jesus removes the stain of your guilt and makes you holy and fit to enter the perfection of his heaven. And your salvation will never be taken away from you.

God also made it quite clear that every person has the freedom to follow Jesus or not. However, anyone who chooses not to is making the tragic decision to spend eternity apart from God. It's not God's desire—it's a personal choice.

* * *

Don't be afraid of those who want to kill your body; they cannot touch your soul. Fear only God, who can destroy both soul and body in hell. MATTHEW 10:28

Q. ARE THERE DIFFERENT LEVELS OF PUNISHMENT IN HELL?

Is there a "sort of" bad place and a "super" bad place?

A. According to the Bible, at the Last Judgment those who have rejected Jesus are thrown into the lake of fire right behind Satan. We don't know if one part of the lake of fire is worse than another part. But there's no doubt that terrible is terrible.

The Bible does teach that people are judged according to their sins, so it may be that there will be worse consequences for some. Jesus taught that a person who knows what to do and doesn't do it will receive a greater degree of punishment than one who doesn't know how to obey (Luke 12:47-48).

The bottom line is that hell is a horrible place of eternal suffering. To prevent those we care about from going there, we should do whatever we can to share with them the truth and love of Jesus.

The Son of Man will send his angels, and they will remove from his Kingdom everything that causes sin and all who do evil. And the angels will throw them into the fiery furnace, where there will be weeping and gnashing of teeth. Then the righteous will shine like the sun in their Father's Kingdom. MATTHEW 13:41-43

88

Q. WILL PEOPLE IN HELL GET ANOTHER CHANCE AT HEAVEN?

If they change their minds about God, will he let them come to heaven?

A. While living, people have many opportunities to recognize their need for Jesus and come to him for salvation. But upon death, if they have not said yes to Jesus, there are no more chances to turn to God.

In Luke 16, Jesus tells a story about a rich man who was sent to hell. The man glimpses the patriarch Abraham in heaven and asks for relief from his anguish. Abraham reminds the man that while he was alive, he had everything he wanted; yet he still hadn't made room in his life for God. Then Abraham delivers the final blow: "Besides, there is a great chasm separating us. No one can cross over to you from here, and no one can cross over to us from there" (verse 26).

The reality of hell is tragic for those who don't accept the gift of forgiveness that Jesus offers. In light of this, can you think of any reason not to give your life to him now? Jesus will never reject those who come to him with humble, repentant hearts. Trust in him, for he loves you more than you can imagine!

Each person is destined to die once and after that comes judgment. HEBREWS 9:27

Q. WHAT ARE "THE END TIMES"?

Are we talking "the end of the world" here?

A. The term *end times* does refer to the end of the world—plus the events leading up to it. The Bible contains vivid descriptions of these events, though their exact meaning has been debated for years. What is clearly understood, however, is that Jesus will return to earth to render judgment and fully establish his Kingdom. Scripture tells us that only God the Father knows when this will happen—not even Jesus knows the day or hour (Matthew 24:36). When people claim to know that Jesus will come on a certain date, they're wrong.

For Christians, the end times are the fulfillment of Jesus' promise of victory over death and the privilege of ruling and reigning with him forever. At the Final Judgment they will receive their just rewards for obeying God. Those who reject God will be condemned to hell, separated forever from God's loving presence. In spite of the cataclysmic events of the end times, those who belong to Jesus can rest in knowing they will share an inheritance in his glorious Kingdom.

○ ○ ○ ○ ○ ● ○ ○ ○ ○ ● ○ ○ ○ ● ○ ○ ● ● ● ○ ○ ○ ○ ○ ● ○ ○

It will happen in a moment, in the blink of an eye, when the last trumpet is blown. For when the trumpet sounds, those who have died will be raised to live forever. And we who are living will also be transformed.   1 CORINTHIANS 15:52

Q. WHERE CAN I READ ABOUT THE END TIMES IN THE BIBLE?

It's kind of scary to think about the end of the world. Does God tell us what is going to happen?

A. Several places in the Bible speak about the end times—Daniel 2 and 7–9, Matthew 24, 2 Peter 3, and most of the book of Revelation. All of these descriptions are worth our attention, but there are a few things to keep in mind.

First, many of them are written in highly symbolic language, and not all Christians agree on what they mean.

Second, Jesus stressed that no one—not even himself—knows when the end times will happen, so people who fixate on it are probably missing the point. It's more important for us to live faithfully in the present than to understand exactly what will happen in the future.

Third, the terrifying descriptions of the end of the world also bring the ultimate good news: Satan will be defeated. Jesus will return in triumph. There will be no more tears, no more sadness—just a big celebration—and then God's children will live forever with him.

○ ○ ○ ○ ○ ○ ○ ○ ○ ○ ● ○ ○ ○ ○ ○ ○ ○ ○ ○ ○ ● ○ ○ ○ ● ○ ○

We are looking forward to the new heavens and new earth he has promised, a world filled with God's righteousness.

2 PETER 3:13

91

Q. WHAT ARE SOME SIGNS THAT THE END TIMES ARE NEAR?

Will we have any warnings?

A. The Bible describes several circumstances that will be signs of the end times. Many sound familiar: wars and threats of war between nations, an increased incidence of earthquakes and famines, and believers suffering persecution at the hands of those who rage against God. Some who claim to be Christians will fall into false beliefs about God, and people will be concerned only about themselves and how much money they can gather. Fortunately, Jesus told us there is at least one encouraging event we can look forward to: The Good News about Jesus will be preached throughout the world so that everyone can hear it.

These will not be pleasant years for both believers and unbelievers. Jesus himself said "there will be greater anguish than at any time since the world began" (Matthew 24:21). So it will be especially important for Jesus' followers to seek God and stay in close fellowship with him and one another. As darkness increases over the earth, God's children will shine even brighter with the light of his love and hope!

When all these things begin to happen, stand and look up, for your salvation is near! LUKE 21:28

Q. HAVE ANY PROPHECIES ABOUT THE END TIMES ALREADY BEEN FULFILLED?

Have some of the predictions about the end already come to pass?

A. Wars, earthquakes, and rampant materialism are certainly realities in our day and time. However, Jesus clarified that these signs are only the beginning of what is to come.

The predictions of what will happen during the end times remind us not to become complacent. The Bible tells us to always be alert and ready because Jesus could come back at any time. And how can we accomplish this? Not by being worried or anxious, but by drawing close to Jesus and staying true to what the Bible teaches as truth.

[Jesus said,] "So you, too, must keep watch! . . . Understand this: If a homeowner knew exactly when a burglar was coming, he would keep watch and not permit his house to be broken into. You also must be ready all the time, for the Son of Man will come when least expected." MATTHEW 24:42-44

Q. HOW CAN I UNDERSTAND THE BOOK OF REVELATION?

The book of Revelation is kind of strange and hard to follow. How can I figure out what it means?

A. People have been studying Revelation—the final book of the Bible—for centuries, yet many today still grapple with understanding the rich imagery in the apostle John's vision. But there is still a lot to glean from its pages. What's most important is to grasp the core message of the book—that the time is coming when Jesus will return to gather his followers and establish his Kingdom.

Revelation is filled with visions of the future and both warnings and encouragement for what is to come. It may not be possible to fully explain the symbolism it encompasses, but it *is* possible to heed its admonishment to accept Jesus as Savior and live faithfully and passionately for him. Such powerful prophecies serve as reminders to share the story of God's love with others so they, too, can inherit his promises.

○ ○ ○ ○ ○ ● ○ ○ ○ ○ ● ○ ○ ○ ○ ○ ● ○ ○ ● ● ○ ○ ○ ○ ○ ○ ● ○ ○

No power in the sky above or in the earth below—indeed, nothing in all creation will ever be able to separate us from the love of God that is revealed in Christ Jesus our Lord. ROMANS 8:39

Q. WILL GOD REALLY JUDGE EVERY PERSON WHO HAS EVER LIVED?

Christians too?

A. It's true the Bible teaches that those who reject Jesus will be judged. Having made the choice to separate themselves from God, they will be sentenced to eternity in hell.

But what about Christians? Will they also be judged? Yes, though not in the same way as those who rebel against God. When someone accepts Jesus as Savior, that person becomes God's child and inherits his promise of eternal life. Yet God's children will still stand before the judgment seat of Christ to give an account for how they lived. Were they obedient to his commands? Did they serve him and show love to others? After answering for these things, they will receive whatever reward is fitting. Now that's motivation for living in a manner that is pleasing to God!

○ ○ ○ ○ ○ ○ ○ ○ ○ ○ ● ○ ○ ● ○ ○ ○ ○ ○ ○ ● ○ ○ ● ○ ○ ○ ○

Each of us will give a personal account to God. ROMANS 14:12

Q. WHY DO CHRISTIANS LOOK FORWARD TO THE END TIMES?

The end times sound awful! Why should I be glad they're coming?

A. Christians look forward to the end times because they lead to the fulfillment of some of Jesus' most wonderful promises. When he returns, he will glorify their earthly bodies, reward their righteous deeds, bring justice to their enemies, and establish God's eternal Kingdom.

There are varying thoughts on how difficult life on earth might be just prior to Jesus' return, but Christians know that God will help them endure. They focus on the joy they will experience when at last Jesus wipes away every tear from their eyes. The hope of his glorious presence filling the earth will overshadow whatever problems the end times may bring.

Christians believe they are never, ever alone, no matter what is going on in their lives or in the world around them. Jesus promised to be with them always, and that is sufficient hope in the midst of any challenge.

Even when I walk through the darkest valley, I will not be afraid, for you are close beside me. PSALM 23:4

Q. WILL JESUS WARN US WHEN HE IS COMING BACK?

Shouldn't we at least have a clue about the timing so we can be ready?

A. The Bible makes it clear that Jesus' coming will catch everyone by surprise. People will be working or playing or sleeping, and suddenly he will be here! We know he's coming, but we don't know when.

Why won't we get a warning? If we knew exactly when Jesus was coming, then we might put off making a decision to believe in him until just before he returns. And that would defeat God's purpose for our lives: knowing him and enjoying his love and guidance over a lifetime. Those who end up waiting until the last minute will miss out on the joys of serving God and answered prayer. It may not seem like it, but lack of a warning is truly a blessing in disguise!

- -

In those days before the flood, the people were enjoying banquets and parties and weddings right up to the time Noah entered his boat. People didn't realize what was going to happen until the flood came and swept them all away. That is the way it will be when the Son of Man comes. MATTHEW 24:38-39

Q. WHY IS JESUS WAITING SO LONG TO COME BACK?

Things in the world keep getting worse and worse. Why hasn't he returned yet?

A. It's been about two thousand years since Jesus promised he would one day come back for his followers. What is taking so long? There are a couple of possible explanations.

One is that God is allowing time for more and more people to hear about his love. His desire is that every person will accept the forgiveness offered by Jesus his Son so they can spend eternity with him.

The second builds on the first: God is also making sure his followers have time to do their jobs and share his love with others. If we love God, we will offer others the opportunity to learn about the plan of salvation. The longer we walk in faith, the more serious we become about this responsibility.

You must not forget this one thing, dear friends: A day is like a thousand years to the Lord, and a thousand years is like a day. The Lord isn't really being slow about his promise, as some people think. No, he is being patient for your sake. He does not want anyone to be destroyed, but wants everyone to repent.

2 PETER 3:8-9

Q. WHAT'S THE BEST WAY TO LIVE WHILE WAITING FOR JESUS' SECOND COMING?

Since I don't know exactly when he is returning, what should I be doing?

A. We may not know exactly when Jesus is coming back, but he's given us plenty to do in the meantime. The best way to live as we wait for his return is to focus on obeying him in the here and now—doing our best to authentically love God and others.

Spend time getting to know God better by reading his Word, the Bible, and learning about what he expects. Worship and praise him as you intercede for others and bring your own personal requests before him in prayer. Put "feet and hands" to your faith by serving others any way you can—feeding and clothing the poor, visiting the sick and the lonely. And share your faith in kindness and love with everyone you meet.

If we make obeying God and living for him the focus of our lives, then we will be ready for Jesus' return.

[Jesus said,] "Not everyone who calls out to me, 'Lord! Lord!' will enter the Kingdom of Heaven. Only those who actually do the will of my Father in heaven will enter." MATTHEW 7:21

Q. WILL EVERYONE SUBMIT TO JESUS WHEN HE COMES BACK?

Some people are so against God that it is hard to believe they will ever acknowledge that Jesus is Lord.

A. The Bible states there will come a time when every single person will bow down to Jesus. Even people who rejected his salvation will be so struck by Jesus' majesty and power that they will drop to their knees and declare him as King. So yes, every person will one day acknowledge that Jesus is God—Messiah and King over all. It may be too late for their salvation, but it won't be too late for them to see the truth.

○ ○ ○ ○ ○ ● ○ ○ ○ ● ○ ○ ○ ○ ○ ●○ ○ ● ● ●○ ○ ○ ○ ○ ● ○ ○

God elevated [Jesus] to the place of highest honor and gave him the name above all other names, that at the name of Jesus every knee should bow, in heaven and on earth and under the earth, and every tongue declare that Jesus Christ is Lord, to the glory of God the Father. PHILIPPIANS 2:9-11

Q. HOW WILL THE END TIMES "END"?

God wins, right?

A. Yes, God wins. That's a certainty. But before that wonderful ending, life on earth will get much, much worse. According to John's vision in Revelation, there will be terrible persecutions, devastating plagues, natural disasters, and violent wars—worse than history has ever known.

Satan will throw everything he has into waging war against God, but when Jesus returns, Satan will be confined to a bottomless pit for a thousand years. After that, he will be released and will attack God's people once more, but that will be his last hurrah. Satan's armies will be consumed by fire from heaven, and Satan himself will be tossed into a lake of fire and eternal torment.

Then comes the Last Judgment, when God will examine the hearts of everyone who ever lived. Those who rejected Jesus will be consigned to hell for eternity, but those who remained faithful to him will be rewarded with eternal salvation and joy in God's Kingdom.

○ ○ ○ ○ ○ ○ ○ ○ ● ● ○ ○ ○ ○ ○ ○ ○ ○ ○ ○ ● ○ ○ ○ ● ○ ○

The one sitting on the throne said . . . "It is finished! I am the Alpha and the Omega—the Beginning and the End. To all who are thirsty I will give freely from the springs of the water of life. All who are victorious will inherit all these blessings, and I will be their God, and they will be my children." REVELATION 21:5-7

Q. WHAT IS THE NEW HEAVEN AND THE NEW EARTH?

Why do we need new ones?

A. After the Final Judgment, God will completely wipe out this sin-tainted earth and replace it with a new heaven and a new earth—completely fresh and clean and beautiful. The new Jerusalem, God's heavenly city, will be central to this new creation.

Have you ever heard people talk about heaven's "pearly gates" and "streets of gold"? The Bible specifically mentions them as part of the new Jerusalem, and believers—in their resurrected bodies—will have the honor of dwelling forever in this beautiful setting. The new heaven and new earth represent the ultimate fulfilment of God's Kingdom, where there will be no sin, sickness, or sorrow of any kind. What a perfect and wonderful eternal home for those who love Jesus!

I saw a new heaven and a new earth, for the old heaven and the old earth had disappeared. And the sea was also gone. And I saw the holy city, the new Jerusalem, coming down from God out of heaven like a bride beautifully dressed for her husband.

REVELATION 21:1-2